The Biweekly Mortgage Payment Strategy Explained

How to Use Simple Payment Adjustments to Pay Off Your Mortgage Years Earlier

By Joseph G. Correa

Copyright & Legal Notice

Published by Live Stronger Faster

First Edition, 2026

Table of Contents

Introduction 5

Chapter 1: Understanding How the Biweekly Mortgage Payment Strategy Really Works....15

Chapter 2: The Hidden Power of Mortgage Amortization and Interest Reduction....32

Chapter 3: Setting Up a Successful Biweekly Mortgage Payment System Without Costly Mistakes....49

Chapter 4: Creating a Long-Term Mortgage Payoff Mindset That Builds Financial Freedom.... 65

Chapter 5: Combining Biweekly Payments with Extra Principal Strategies for Maximum Acceleration....78

Chapter 6: Avoiding Common Mortgage Payoff Mistakes That Can Slow Your Financial Progress.... 93

Chapter 7: Using Income Growth and Cash Flow Increases to Accelerate Mortgage Freedom....109

Chapter 8: How to Stay Motivated During the Long Mortgage Payoff Journey.... 124

Chapter 9: Balancing Mortgage Payoff with Investing and Long-Term Wealth Building....140

Chapter 10: The Ultimate Mortgage Payoff Game Plan: Combining All Strategies Into Financial Freedom....158

Final Tips and Suggestions for Mortgage Freedom....171

Introduction ... 5

Chapter 1: Understanding How the Biweekly Mortgage Payment Strategy Really Works ... 6

Chapter 2: The Hidden Power of Mortgage Amortization and Interest Reduction ... 32

Chapter 3: Setting Up a Successful Biweekly Mortgage Payment System Without Costly Mistakes ... 49

Chapter 4: Creating a Long-Term Mortgage Payoff Mindset That Builds Financial Freedom ... 64

Chapter 5: Combining Biweekly Payments with Extra Principal Strategies for Maximum Acceleration ... 76

Chapter 6: Avoiding Common Mortgage Payoff Mistakes That Can Slow Your Financial Progress ... 93

Chapter 7: Using Income Growth and Cash Flow Increases to Accelerate Mortgage Freedom ... 109

Chapter 8: How to Stay Motivated During the Long Mortgage Payoff Journey ... 124

Chapter 9: Balancing Mortgage Payoff with Investing and Long-Term Wealth Building ... 140

Chapter 10: The Ultimate Mortgage Payoff Game Plan: Combining All Strategies Into Financial Freedom ... 158

Final Tips and Suggestions for Mortgage Freedom ... 171

Introduction

For most homeowners, the mortgage is the single largest debt they will ever carry in their lifetime. It is a long-term financial commitment that often stretches across fifteen, twenty, or even thirty years. While owning a home is one of the most powerful ways to build wealth and stability, the reality is that many people spend hundreds of thousands of dollars in interest over the life of their loan without ever fully understanding how their mortgage actually works. Most borrowers focus only on the monthly payment. They simply want to know whether the payment fits within their budget. Yet hidden inside every mortgage payment is an opportunity—an opportunity to reduce years of debt, save massive amounts of interest, and accelerate financial freedom far faster than most people ever imagine possible.

One of the simplest and most effective strategies for accomplishing this is the biweekly mortgage payment strategy. Unlike risky investments, complicated financial products, or aggressive debt payoff systems that require major sacrifices, the biweekly payment method works through consistency, timing, and mathematics. It is a strategy that can quietly shave years off a mortgage while potentially saving tens or even hundreds of thousands of dollars in interest payments over time. The beauty of this approach is that it does not require a second job, extreme budgeting, or radical lifestyle changes. Instead, it works by slightly adjusting the rhythm of how mortgage payments are made.

Most homeowners are taught to think in monthly cycles because mortgages are traditionally billed once per month. However, many people are actually paid every two weeks. This creates a disconnect between income timing and debt repayment timing. The biweekly mortgage strategy closes that gap by aligning mortgage payments more closely with income frequency. By doing this, borrowers create a subtle but powerful acceleration effect that compounds over time. Small adjustments begin creating large long-term results.

The concept itself sounds simple on the surface. Instead of making one full mortgage payment every month, the homeowner makes half of the payment every two weeks. Because there are fifty-two weeks in a year, this results in twenty-six half-payments annually, which equals thirteen full payments instead of twelve. That extra payment each year goes directly toward reducing the principal balance of the mortgage. Once the principal balance decreases, interest calculations begin shrinking as well. This creates a chain reaction that accelerates the loan payoff schedule. What makes this strategy remarkable is how accessible it is to ordinary people. Many financial strategies are reserved for high-income earners, experienced investors, or people with advanced financial knowledge. The biweekly mortgage strategy is different. It can work for teachers, nurses, business owners, construction workers, first-time homebuyers, retirees, and families living on moderate incomes. It is not about financial complexity. It is about financial consistency.

The average homeowner often assumes that paying off a mortgage early requires sacrificing everything enjoyable in life. Many people believe they must eliminate vacations, stop dining out, avoid hobbies, or live under constant financial pressure to become debt-free sooner. While discipline is certainly important, the truth is that intelligent financial systems often outperform emotional extremes. Sustainable strategies tend to create better long-term results than aggressive short-term sacrifices that people cannot maintain. This is one of the reasons the biweekly strategy has become so popular among financially disciplined homeowners who want steady progress without destroying their quality of life.

In today's economy, financial freedom has become more important than ever. Inflation, rising living costs, job uncertainty, and market volatility have caused many people to rethink how they manage debt. The idea of carrying a mortgage payment for thirty years can feel overwhelming, especially when homeowners begin calculating how much interest they will ultimately pay. For many borrowers, a thirty-year mortgage may cost nearly double the original purchase price once interest is included. This realization motivates people to search for ways to regain control over their financial future.

Mortgage debt itself is not inherently bad. In fact, real estate ownership has historically been one of the strongest paths toward wealth creation. However, unnecessary interest payments can dramatically slow financial progress. Every dollar paid toward interest is a dollar that cannot be invested, saved, or used to improve quality of life. Reducing interest expenses allows homeowners to redirect cash flow toward retirement accounts, businesses, investments, travel, education, family goals, or future opportunities.

One of the biggest advantages of the biweekly strategy is psychological momentum. Financial progress often becomes easier when people can visibly see debt shrinking faster. Traditional mortgages can sometimes feel discouraging because early payments are heavily weighted toward interest rather than principal reduction. Many homeowners become frustrated after years of payments with only modest reductions in their loan balance. The biweekly strategy changes this dynamic by accelerating principal reduction earlier in the loan term. This can create a stronger sense of motivation and progress.

Another important benefit is the potential improvement in financial flexibility over time. As the mortgage balance decreases faster, homeowners build equity more rapidly. Increased equity creates opportunities. It may allow access to better refinancing options, lower loan-to-value ratios, improved borrowing terms, or future real estate investments. Faster equity growth can also provide emotional security during uncertain economic periods because homeowners gain a stronger ownership position in their property.

This book is designed to provide far more than a simple explanation of how biweekly payments work. It is intended to help you fully understand the mechanics behind mortgage amortization, interest calculations, principal reduction, and payoff acceleration. Once you understand the system, you can begin making smarter decisions that align with your financial goals rather than blindly following traditional payment structures.

Throughout this book, you will learn how mortgage interest compounds over time and why the timing of payments matters more than most people realize. You will discover how even small additional payments toward principal can dramatically shorten a loan term. You will also learn how to structure biweekly payments correctly to avoid common mistakes and unnecessary fees that some lenders or third-party companies may charge.

Many homeowners are surprised to discover that some "biweekly payment programs" offered by outside companies are unnecessary and sometimes expensive. Certain services charge enrollment fees or monthly maintenance fees simply to process payments that borrowers could often manage themselves. Part of becoming financially empowered is learning how to identify efficient strategies while avoiding unnecessary costs. This book will help you distinguish between genuine value and unnecessary complexity.

You will also explore how the biweekly strategy can be adapted to different financial situations. Every borrower is unique. Some people have stable salaried income, while others are self-employed or work with irregular cash flow. Some homeowners prioritize aggressive debt elimination, while others prefer balancing mortgage payoff with investing. There is no one-size-fits-all financial strategy. Instead, the goal is to build a personalized system that supports both wealth growth and financial peace of mind.

One of the most overlooked aspects of mortgage payoff

strategies is behavior. Mathematics alone does not determine financial success. Human habits, emotions, discipline, and consistency often matter even more. Many people understand basic financial principles but struggle with implementation because they lack systems that fit their lifestyle. Sustainable financial habits are usually built through automation, simplicity, and gradual progress rather than extreme financial pressure.

The biweekly strategy works particularly well because it naturally encourages discipline without feeling overwhelming. Smaller, more frequent payments often feel psychologically easier to manage than large lump sums. Additionally, because the extra annual payment is spread across the year, many homeowners barely notice the difference in their monthly cash flow. Yet over time, the long-term impact becomes substantial.

As you move through this book, you will see detailed examples showing how different loan amounts, interest rates, and payment structures affect mortgage payoff timelines. You will begin to understand how lenders earn money through long-term interest accumulation and why reducing principal earlier creates such a powerful financial advantage for borrowers. Knowledge creates leverage, and leverage creates options.

You will also learn that paying off a mortgage faster is not solely about becoming debt-free. It is about reclaiming financial control. A homeowner without a mortgage payment often gains dramatically increased flexibility in life. Monthly expenses decrease. Savings rates can increase. Retirement planning becomes easier. Career choices may become more flexible. Stress levels often decline. The absence of a mortgage payment can fundamentally change a household's financial trajectory.

However, this book will also approach the topic with balance and realism. Accelerating mortgage payoff is not always the correct decision in every situation. There are times when investing excess cash elsewhere may create higher long-term returns. There are situations where maintaining liquidity is more important than aggressively reducing debt. Financial decisions should always be made within the context of personal goals, risk tolerance, income stability, tax considerations, and long-term wealth strategies.

This series is not about blindly promoting one financial philosophy over another. It is about empowering you with the tools, knowledge, and strategies necessary to make intelligent decisions with confidence. The biweekly mortgage payment strategy is one tool among many, but it is one of the most powerful foundational techniques available because of its simplicity, accessibility, and long-term impact.

Financial freedom rarely happens overnight. Instead, it is usually built through consistent actions repeated over many years. Small improvements in financial behavior can produce extraordinary outcomes when compounded over time. Just as interest compounds for lenders, disciplined financial habits can compound for borrowers. The goal is to shift the system in your favor.

By reading this book, you are already taking an important step toward greater financial awareness and control. Most people never study how mortgages truly function. They simply make payments for decades without realizing they may have options to accelerate their progress. Education changes that. Once you understand the mechanics behind your mortgage, you begin seeing opportunities that were previously invisible.

The journey toward mortgage freedom is not merely about numbers on a balance sheet. It is about creating stability, reducing stress, increasing opportunity, and building a life with greater flexibility and confidence. Whether your goal is to eliminate debt early, create more cash flow, retire comfortably, invest in additional properties, or simply achieve peace of mind, the strategies in this book can help move you closer to those objectives.

The biweekly mortgage payment strategy may appear simple at first glance, but its long-term power can be extraordinary when applied consistently and intelligently. Over the coming chapters, you will discover how this strategy works, why it works, how to implement it effectively, and how to combine it with broader wealth-building principles to create lasting financial acceleration.

Your mortgage does not have to control your life for the next thirty years. With the right knowledge, structure, and discipline, you can begin taking control of the timeline, reducing unnecessary interest, and building a stronger financial future starting today.

Chapter 1

Understanding How the Biweekly Mortgage Payment Strategy Really Works

Most homeowners spend years making mortgage payments without fully understanding how their loan actually functions behind the scenes. They know the amount due each month, the interest rate attached to the loan, and perhaps the number of years remaining until payoff. Yet very few borrowers truly understand how the timing of payments impacts the total interest paid over the life of the mortgage. This lack of understanding often causes homeowners to miss opportunities that could potentially save them years of debt and significant amounts of money. One of the most powerful and accessible opportunities available is the biweekly mortgage payment strategy.

At first glance, the concept may appear almost too simple to make a meaningful difference. Many borrowers initially assume that changing the frequency of mortgage payments cannot possibly create major financial results. However, mortgage mathematics works differently than most people realize. Small adjustments in payment structure can create large long-term effects because of the way interest is calculated and principal balances decline over time.

To fully understand the biweekly mortgage strategy, it is important to first understand how a traditional mortgage payment works. In a standard mortgage structure, the borrower makes one payment every month. This payment is divided into several portions, including principal, interest, taxes, and insurance if escrow is included. The principal portion reduces the loan balance, while the interest portion represents the lender's profit for borrowing the money.

One of the most important realities about mortgages is that interest is heavily front-loaded during the early years of the loan. In the beginning stages of a thirty-year mortgage, a large percentage of the payment goes toward interest rather than principal reduction. This means homeowners often spend years making payments while seeing only modest reductions in their actual loan balance. Many borrowers become frustrated when they realize how slowly equity builds during the first several years.

For example, imagine a homeowner with a $400,000 mortgage at a 7% interest rate over thirty years. The monthly principal and interest payment may be approximately $2,661. During the first payment, a large portion goes toward interest while only a smaller amount reduces the principal balance. Although the homeowner may feel they are making significant progress, the lender continues earning substantial interest income month after month.

The lender's advantage comes from time. The longer the loan remains outstanding, the more interest the lender collects. This is why accelerating principal reduction earlier in the loan term becomes so powerful. Once the principal balance begins shrinking faster, the amount of interest charged also begins decreasing. This creates a compounding acceleration effect that can dramatically shorten the mortgage timeline.

The biweekly mortgage strategy takes advantage of this concept through payment frequency. Instead of making one full mortgage payment every month, the borrower makes half of the payment every two weeks. Since there are fifty-two weeks in a year, this results in twenty-six half-payments annually. Twenty-six half-payments equal thirteen full payments instead of twelve.

That single extra payment each year becomes the key to the strategy. Because the extra payment is applied toward principal reduction, it directly lowers the outstanding mortgage balance faster than the original amortization schedule intended. Once the balance decreases, future interest calculations also decline. Over time, this creates substantial savings.

To better understand the impact, consider a homeowner making a standard monthly mortgage payment of $2,400. Under a traditional payment structure, they make twelve payments annually for a total of $28,800 per year. Under a biweekly structure, they would pay $1,200 every two weeks. Over the course of the year, twenty-six half-payments equal $31,200 annually. The difference is $2,400, which equals one extra monthly payment.

That extra payment may not sound life-changing at first, but over time it becomes extremely powerful. Depending on the loan amount and interest rate, the strategy may reduce a thirty-year mortgage by four to six years or more. It may also save tens of thousands of dollars in interest payments. The higher the loan amount and interest rate, the greater the long-term savings may become.

One reason this strategy works well psychologically is because the extra payment feels manageable. Instead of trying to make one large additional payment at the end of the year, the borrower spreads the extra amount across the entire year. Smaller incremental payments often feel easier emotionally and financially than large lump sums. This makes the strategy sustainable for many households. Another important benefit is that the strategy aligns naturally with how many people receive income. A large percentage of workers are paid every two weeks rather than once per month. Traditional monthly mortgages can create awkward timing issues where borrowers receive paychecks biweekly but must manage a large monthly payment cycle. The biweekly strategy creates stronger alignment between income frequency and debt repayment frequency.

Automation also plays a major role in the success of this strategy. Many borrowers who automate their biweekly payments discover that consistency becomes easier because they remove emotional decision-making from the process. Automatic payments create financial discipline without requiring constant effort. Over time, disciplined automation often produces better results than relying solely on motivation.

However, homeowners must also understand the difference between true biweekly payments and simple "twice-per-month" payments. These are not always the same thing. A true biweekly payment occurs every fourteen days, resulting in twenty-six half-payments annually. A semi-monthly payment structure usually involves making payments twice per month, such as on the 1st and 15th. Semi-monthly structures often result in only twenty-four half-payments annually, which equals twelve full payments rather than thirteen. This distinction matters because the extra annual payment drives much of the strategy's acceleration effect. Borrowers should verify how their lender processes payments before assuming they are receiving the full benefit of a biweekly structure. Understanding the details prevents confusion and ensures the strategy functions properly.

Some lenders officially offer biweekly payment programs, while others do not. In certain cases, homeowners may choose to create the system themselves by manually making additional principal payments. For example, a borrower may continue making monthly payments but add one-twelfth of an extra payment toward principal each month. This can produce a similar long-term effect without requiring a formal biweekly setup.

Unfortunately, many third-party companies attempt to profit from homeowners by charging fees to manage biweekly payment programs. Some services charge enrollment fees, monthly processing fees, or administrative costs that reduce the financial benefit of the strategy. Homeowners should carefully evaluate whether such services are necessary. In many situations, borrowers can implement similar strategies independently without paying outside companies.

Understanding mortgage amortization is essential for appreciating why the biweekly strategy works so effectively. Amortization refers to the gradual reduction of debt through scheduled payments over time. In the early years of a mortgage, interest dominates the payment structure because the loan balance is highest at the beginning. As the balance declines, more of each payment begins going toward principal reduction.

When borrowers make additional principal payments early in the loan term, they disrupt the original amortization schedule. Even small extra payments can create major long-term savings because they reduce future interest calculations across many remaining years of the loan. Time magnifies the impact of early principal reduction.

For example, reducing a mortgage balance by even a few thousand dollars during the first five years may eliminate interest charges that would have accumulated over decades. This is why timing matters so much. Extra payments made early in the mortgage often produce greater savings than the same payments made later in the loan term.

The biweekly strategy also creates momentum. Financial progress tends to reinforce positive behavior. As homeowners begin seeing their principal balance shrink faster, they often become more motivated to continue improving their finances. Some borrowers eventually combine the biweekly strategy with other acceleration methods such as lump-sum payments, refinancing strategies, rental income, side businesses, or investment income.

Another important advantage is flexibility. The biweekly strategy can often be adjusted based on changing financial circumstances. During stronger income periods, borrowers may increase extra principal payments. During more difficult periods, they may temporarily scale back to standard payment structures if necessary. Financial systems that allow flexibility tend to be more sustainable long term.

It is also important to recognize that paying off a mortgage early is not solely about mathematics. Emotional security plays a major role. Many homeowners experience tremendous peace of mind knowing they are steadily reducing debt faster than expected. The psychological relief associated with debt reduction can positively impact relationships, career choices, retirement planning, and overall stress levels.

At the same time, homeowners should maintain balance and avoid becoming financially overextended in pursuit of rapid payoff. Emergency savings, retirement planning, liquidity, and overall financial stability remain important. Accelerating mortgage payoff should complement broader financial goals rather than create unnecessary hardship.

The biweekly strategy works best when integrated into a complete financial plan. Some borrowers may prioritize aggressive payoff, while others may balance debt reduction with investing opportunities. There is no universally perfect approach. Financial decisions should reflect personal goals, income stability, risk tolerance, and long-term priorities.

What makes the biweekly strategy especially attractive is its simplicity. Many financial systems fail because they are overly complicated or difficult to maintain consistently. Simplicity increases sustainability. A strategy that homeowners can realistically follow for years often produces far greater results than aggressive plans abandoned after a few months.

As this book continues, you will explore advanced examples, mortgage payoff projections, amortization concepts, and additional acceleration techniques that can work alongside biweekly payments. You will begin developing a deeper understanding of how mortgages operate and how small financial adjustments can create major long-term wealth benefits.

Ultimately, the biweekly mortgage payment strategy is about reclaiming control over the timeline of debt. Instead of allowing a thirty-year mortgage to dictate decades of interest payments, homeowners can begin shifting the system in their favor. Through consistency, discipline, and strategic payment timing, it becomes possible to accelerate equity growth, reduce interest expenses, and move closer to long-term financial freedom.

The Family That Quietly Eliminated 8 Years of Mortgage Payments

When Carlos and Elena Ramirez bought their first home, they felt proud, relieved, and slightly terrified all at the same time. After years of renting small apartments throughout central Florida, they had finally purchased a modest three-bedroom home in a quiet suburban neighborhood where their children could play safely outside. To them, the house represented stability, family, and the beginning of a better future.

Like many first-time homeowners, they focused primarily on getting approved for the loan and making sure the monthly payment fit within their budget. The mortgage broker explained the interest rate, escrow account, and closing costs, but neither Carlos nor Elena spent much time thinking about the long-term structure of the mortgage itself. Thirty years sounded normal because almost everyone they knew had a thirty-year loan.

Carlos worked as an HVAC technician, while Elena managed a small dental office. Together, they earned enough to live comfortably but not extravagantly. After paying the mortgage, utilities, groceries, insurance, childcare, and gas, there was not a huge amount left over every month. They were careful with money, but they did not feel wealthy. For the first two years, they made their mortgage payment every month like clockwork. Each payment felt significant because it represented one of the largest expenses in their lives. Yet one evening, Elena logged into their mortgage account and noticed something discouraging. Despite making payments for over two years, the loan balance had barely decreased.

"How is that possible?" she asked while staring at the screen.

Carlos leaned over the kitchen table and looked at the numbers. "We've paid over sixty thousand dollars already," he said. "Why does it feel like we still owe almost everything?"

Neither of them fully understood amortization at the time. Most of their payments had gone toward interest during the early years of the loan. The realization frustrated them. They began wondering whether they would truly spend thirty years paying for the house.

A few weeks later, Carlos was talking with an older customer while repairing an air conditioning system. During the conversation, the homeowner casually mentioned that he had paid off his mortgage nearly seven years early using biweekly payments.

Carlos had never heard of the strategy before.

"What do you mean biweekly payments?" he asked.

The man smiled. "Simple. Instead of paying once a month, I paid half every two weeks. Doesn't sound like much, but over time it changes everything."

That evening Carlos researched the strategy online and began running mortgage calculators. The numbers surprised him. If they switched to biweekly payments, they could potentially save tens of thousands of dollars in interest and eliminate several years from their loan.

When he explained it to Elena, she looked skeptical at first.

"So we just split the payment in half?" she asked.

"Basically," Carlos said. "But because there are twenty-six biweekly periods in a year, it ends up being one extra payment annually."

Elena grabbed a notebook and started calculating the numbers herself. The more they reviewed the math, the more excited they became. The strategy did not require a second job, huge sacrifices, or risky investments. It simply required consistency.

They decided to test the approach for six months.

Because Elena was paid biweekly already, the adjustment felt natural. Every paycheck cycle, they transferred half the mortgage payment immediately into a separate account dedicated to housing expenses. Soon, the process became automatic.

At first, they barely noticed the difference.

The extra payment amount was spread across the year, so it did not feel overwhelming. Yet every few months, they checked their mortgage balance and noticed something encouraging. The principal was shrinking slightly faster than before.

That progress motivated them.

Instead of increasing their lifestyle every time they received extra income, they became more intentional. Tax refunds, work bonuses, and occasional side income from Elena helping local businesses with bookkeeping were partially directed toward extra principal payments.

Within three years, they had created financial momentum.

Their mortgage balance had dropped much faster than the original schedule projected. More importantly, they felt psychologically different about money. Instead of feeling trapped by debt, they felt increasingly in control.

The experience changed how they viewed financial decisions overall. They became more cautious about unnecessary spending. They built a stronger emergency fund. They stopped financing furniture and electronics unnecessarily. They focused more on long-term stability than short-term appearances.

As the years passed, something unexpected happened. Their reduced mortgage balance created opportunities.

When interest rates eventually dropped, they qualified for a refinance with better terms because they had built equity faster than many homeowners around them. The refinance lowered their interest rate and accelerated their payoff timeline even further.

Meanwhile, several of their friends continued struggling financially despite earning similar incomes. Many upgraded vehicles frequently, accumulated credit card debt, or increased spending every time their salaries rose. Carlos and Elena realized that wealth was often less about income and more about consistent financial habits.

Their children also began absorbing these lessons.

Family conversations gradually shifted away from consumerism and toward ownership, investing, and financial freedom. The mortgage payoff journey became more than just a financial strategy. It became part of the family culture.

One evening, about twelve years after purchasing the house, Carlos logged into their mortgage account again.

He stared silently at the screen.

"What is it?" Elena asked from across the room.

Carlos smiled slowly. "We're ahead by almost eight years."

Elena walked over and looked at the numbers herself. The realization hit both of them emotionally. They had not achieved this through extreme wealth, lottery winnings, or dramatic sacrifices. They achieved it through steady discipline and small repeated actions over time.

The remaining mortgage balance no longer felt overwhelming. Instead, it felt temporary.

For the first time since buying the house, they could clearly envision life without a mortgage payment.

They began talking about future possibilities. Elena wanted to reduce her office hours eventually. Carlos dreamed about starting his own small HVAC company. They also wanted to help their children avoid financial mistakes many young adults make.

Years later, when they finally paid off the mortgage completely, the moment felt surreal.

There was no massive celebration. No luxury vacation. No dramatic announcement.

Instead, there was quiet peace.

The absence of a mortgage payment changed everything. Monthly cash flow increased dramatically overnight. Stress levels declined. Savings accelerated. Investment contributions increased. Their financial decisions became driven by opportunity rather than obligation.

Carlos often reflected on how simple the original strategy had been.

Most people search for complicated financial secrets, but their breakthrough came from understanding one basic concept: small consistent actions create massive long-term results.

The biweekly mortgage strategy had not magically transformed them into millionaires overnight. What it did was far more important. It gave them control. It shortened the timeline of debt. It increased flexibility. It reduced financial pressure. And perhaps most importantly, it changed the way they thought about money forever.

Years later, when friends or younger coworkers asked Carlos for financial advice, he often smiled and shared the same lesson the older homeowner once shared with him during that air conditioning repair appointment.

"It may seem small at first," he would say. "But consistency changes everything."

Chapter 2

The Hidden Power of Mortgage Amortization and Interest Reduction

Most homeowners spend years making mortgage payments without ever studying the amortization schedule attached to their loan. They know the amount due every month, they understand the interest rate in general terms, and they focus primarily on whether the payment fits within their household budget. However, buried beneath every mortgage payment is a financial structure that determines exactly how much wealth will either remain in the homeowner's pocket or flow into the lender's hands over time. Understanding mortgage amortization is one of the most important steps toward taking control of long-term financial outcomes.

The word amortization may sound complicated or intimidating at first, but the concept itself is relatively simple. Mortgage amortization refers to the process of gradually paying off a loan through scheduled payments over a specific period of time. Each payment contains two primary components: principal and interest. The principal reduces the amount borrowed, while the interest represents the lender's profit for financing the loan. What surprises many borrowers is how uneven this payment structure becomes during the early years of a mortgage. Most people assume that every payment reduces the balance significantly from the beginning. In reality, early mortgage payments are heavily weighted toward interest. This means homeowners may spend years making payments while seeing only slow progress in reducing the actual loan balance.

For example, consider a homeowner with a $500,000 mortgage at a 7% interest rate on a thirty-year fixed loan. The monthly principal and interest payment may exceed $3,300. Yet during the first payment, only a relatively small portion goes toward reducing the principal balance. The majority of the payment flows directly to the lender as interest income.

This imbalance exists because mortgage interest is calculated based on the outstanding loan balance. Since the balance is highest at the beginning of the loan term, interest charges are also highest during that period. As the principal gradually declines, future interest charges slowly decrease as well. This creates a shifting relationship between interest and principal over time.

In the early years, homeowners often feel frustrated when they realize how slowly equity builds. After making payments for several years, some borrowers are shocked to discover they still owe nearly the original loan amount. This frustration is common because most people are never taught how mortgage amortization truly works.

Lenders benefit tremendously from long loan terms because time allows interest accumulation to compound in their favor. A thirty-year mortgage can generate hundreds of thousands of dollars in interest over its lifetime. While the home itself may appreciate in value, borrowers who follow the original amortization schedule often pay far more than they initially expected once interest is included.

Understanding this reality changes how homeowners think about debt. Once borrowers recognize how much interest flows to the lender over time, they begin searching for strategies that reduce the loan balance faster. This is where mortgage acceleration techniques such as biweekly payments become extremely powerful.

The hidden strength of the biweekly strategy lies in its effect on amortization. Every extra dollar applied toward principal directly interrupts the lender's long-term interest calculations. Once principal decreases, future interest charges decline as well. This creates a ripple effect that compounds over many years.

Imagine two homeowners with identical mortgages. The first homeowner follows the standard thirty-year schedule without making extra payments. The second homeowner uses a biweekly strategy that results in one extra payment annually. At first, the difference between the two borrowers appears small. However, over time, the second borrower steadily reduces principal faster, causing future interest charges to shrink.

As the years pass, the gap between the two loan balances grows wider. Eventually, the borrower using the acceleration strategy may eliminate several years of mortgage payments while saving a substantial amount in interest expenses. This demonstrates the power of small, consistent financial adjustments.

One of the most important concepts homeowners must understand is that mortgage interest savings are often greatest when extra payments are made early in the loan term. Timing matters because early principal reductions prevent future interest from accumulating across many remaining years.

For example, applying an additional $5,000 toward principal during the second year of a mortgage may save far more interest than applying the same amount during the twenty-fifth year. The earlier the principal reduction occurs, the longer the borrower benefits from reduced interest calculations.

This principle explains why consistent acceleration strategies are so effective. Homeowners do not necessarily need massive amounts of extra cash to create meaningful results. Small repeated payments made consistently over time can produce extraordinary long-term savings because of how amortization works.

Another reason amortization matters is because it affects psychological motivation. Traditional mortgage schedules often feel discouraging because borrowers see slow progress in the beginning. Many people lose motivation because they believe their payments are accomplishing very little. Accelerated payoff strategies create visible momentum by increasing principal reduction earlier in the process.

Momentum is extremely important in personal finance. People are more likely to maintain positive financial habits when they can visibly see results. As borrowers watch their principal balance decline faster, they often become more disciplined in other areas of their finances as well.

Some homeowners eventually begin combining multiple acceleration techniques together. They may use biweekly payments, occasional lump-sum reductions, annual bonuses, tax refunds, rental income, or side business earnings to further accelerate principal reduction. Once homeowners understand how amortization functions, they begin viewing extra principal payments as investments in future financial freedom.

It is also important to understand that interest savings create additional opportunity costs. Every dollar spent on mortgage interest is a dollar unavailable for investing, retirement contributions, business growth, education, travel, or lifestyle improvements. Reducing unnecessary interest expenses increases future flexibility.

For many families, eliminating a mortgage payment years earlier than expected can dramatically transform their financial lives. Without a mortgage payment, monthly obligations decline substantially. This can create freedom to reduce work hours, retire earlier, pursue entrepreneurship, invest more aggressively, or simply experience less financial stress.

However, homeowners must balance mortgage acceleration with other financial priorities. While reducing debt is valuable, maintaining emergency savings and financial stability remains equally important. Some borrowers become so focused on aggressive payoff that they neglect liquidity and flexibility. Financial acceleration should strengthen stability rather than create unnecessary hardship.

The emotional side of mortgage debt is often underestimated. Debt creates pressure because it represents long-term obligation. Even financially successful individuals sometimes feel psychological stress carrying large mortgage balances for decades. Accelerated payoff strategies can create emotional relief in addition to financial benefits. At the same time, not every homeowner should prioritize mortgage payoff above all else. Certain individuals may benefit more from investing excess funds into appreciating assets, retirement accounts, or businesses capable of generating higher long-term returns. The correct approach depends on personal goals, risk tolerance, age, income stability, and broader financial objectives.

Still, understanding amortization gives homeowners power regardless of which strategy they ultimately choose. Knowledge removes uncertainty. Once borrowers understand how mortgages operate mathematically, they gain the ability to make intentional financial decisions rather than blindly following default loan structures.

Another important aspect of amortization is recognizing how refinancing affects the loan timeline. Some homeowners repeatedly refinance into new thirty-year mortgages, unintentionally resetting their amortization schedule each time. Although refinancing can reduce monthly payments or interest rates, extending the loan term may increase total interest costs if borrowers are not careful.

This does not mean refinancing is inherently bad. In many cases, refinancing can be an excellent financial tool. However, homeowners must understand how amortization resets when making such decisions. Intelligent refinancing strategies often involve balancing interest savings with shorter loan terms or accelerated payoff plans.

Technology has also made mortgage education more accessible than ever before. Online amortization calculators allow homeowners to model different payoff scenarios instantly. Borrowers can now see exactly how extra payments affect interest savings and payoff timelines. These tools help transform abstract financial concepts into visible projections that motivate action.

Many borrowers experience a major mindset shift once they begin analyzing amortization schedules closely. They stop viewing mortgage payments as fixed obligations and start seeing them as flexible financial systems that can be strategically managed. This shift often becomes the foundation for broader financial improvement.

The hidden power of amortization lies in understanding that time can either work against the borrower or for the borrower.

Left untouched, long-term interest accumulation primarily benefits the lender. However, once homeowners begin accelerating principal reduction strategically, time begins shifting in their favor.

Small actions repeated consistently create extraordinary outcomes because compound effects grow larger over time. Just as compound interest helps investments grow, accelerated principal reduction compounds debt elimination progress. The earlier homeowners begin, the stronger the long-term results often become.

Ultimately, understanding mortgage amortization is about far more than numbers. It is about control. Homeowners who understand how interest functions gain the ability to reshape their financial future intentionally rather than passively accepting decades of unnecessary debt costs.

The biweekly strategy works because it harnesses the mechanics of amortization rather than fighting against them. Instead of allowing interest to dominate the loan for decades, borrowers begin reducing principal faster and shrinking future interest calculations simultaneously. This simple shift creates long-term acceleration that can transform financial outcomes.

As you continue through this book, you will discover additional methods for optimizing mortgage payoff, reducing interest expenses, and building financial flexibility. But all of these strategies begin with one foundational truth: once you understand how amortization works, you begin seeing opportunities for wealth acceleration everywhere.

The Teacher Who Discovered Where Her Mortgage Money Was Really Going

Melissa Turner had always considered herself financially responsible. She paid her bills on time, avoided credit card debt whenever possible, contributed modestly to her retirement account, and carefully tracked her monthly spending. As a high school teacher, she understood the importance of discipline and planning because her income required careful budgeting.

When Melissa bought her first home at age thirty-six, she felt proud of herself. The small two-story house was not luxurious, but it represented stability and independence after years of renting apartments while working her way through graduate school and teaching full time.

Her mortgage payment was manageable, though still intimidating. Every month she transferred nearly $2,700 toward the mortgage company, believing she was steadily building ownership in her home. She rarely questioned the process because making monthly mortgage payments simply felt like a normal part of adulthood.

For the first several years, Melissa focused primarily on maintaining financial stability. She furnished the house slowly, completed small home improvement projects herself, and avoided overspending. Friends often joked that she was overly cautious with money, but Melissa preferred peace of mind over financial chaos.

One rainy Saturday afternoon, Melissa sat at her kitchen table reviewing her annual mortgage statement. She had recently attended a teacher retirement workshop that encouraged participants to analyze long-term financial obligations more carefully. Curious about her progress, she logged into her mortgage account and reviewed the remaining balance.

What she saw immediately unsettled her.

Despite making payments faithfully for over four years, her mortgage balance had barely dropped compared to the original loan amount.

"That can't be right," she whispered to herself.

She grabbed a calculator and began adding up her payments over the years. The total amount she had paid toward the mortgage was enormous. Yet when she compared that figure to the actual reduction in her principal balance, she felt almost sick.

Most of her money had gone toward interest.

Melissa spent the rest of the afternoon researching mortgage amortization online. The more she learned, the more frustrated she became. She realized that during the early years of the loan, the lender was collecting the majority of each payment as profit while only a small percentage reduced the actual debt.

For the first time, she truly understood how mortgages worked.

The discovery changed her perspective entirely.

She was not angry at the lender because she understood she had agreed to the terms. However, she suddenly realized that if she continued following the standard payment schedule for thirty years, she would pay an astonishing amount in interest.

That realization motivated her to search for alternatives.

A few days later, Melissa met her longtime friend Rebecca for coffee after work. Rebecca worked as an accountant and had always enjoyed discussing personal finance topics.

"I think I've been completely misunderstanding my mortgage," Melissa admitted.

Rebecca laughed softly. "Most people do."

Melissa explained what she had discovered about amortization and interest-heavy early payments. Rebecca nodded knowingly. "That's why extra principal payments matter so much early on," Rebecca explained. "The earlier you reduce the balance, the more future interest disappears."

Melissa leaned forward. "But I don't have huge amounts of extra money lying around."

"You don't necessarily need huge amounts," Rebecca replied. "Consistency matters more than perfection."

Rebecca then introduced Melissa to the biweekly payment strategy.

At first, Melissa assumed the strategy sounded too simple to matter. But Rebecca showed her several mortgage payoff calculators online. Together they modeled Melissa's loan using biweekly payments instead of standard monthly payments.

The projections shocked her.

Simply by restructuring the payment schedule and effectively making one extra payment annually, she could potentially eliminate years from her mortgage and save tens of thousands of dollars in interest.

For the first time since buying the house, Melissa felt a sense of control.

The following month she reorganized her finances carefully. Since she was paid biweekly already, the transition felt manageable. She automated half of her mortgage payment to transfer every paycheck cycle into a dedicated housing account.

The adjustment was small enough that it did not disrupt her lifestyle dramatically. She still enjoyed dinners with friends occasionally, continued contributing modestly to savings, and maintained her normal routines. The difference was simply that she became more intentional.

Months passed.

Melissa checked her mortgage amortization progress regularly. Gradually, she noticed her principal balance declining slightly faster than before. The changes were not dramatic overnight, but they were consistent.

Consistency created motivation.

Soon she began applying additional small amounts toward principal whenever possible. Summer tutoring income, tax refunds, and extra pay from supervising school activities all became opportunities to accelerate progress.

As her mortgage balance declined faster, Melissa noticed something unexpected happening emotionally.

Her anxiety about money began decreasing.

For years she had viewed her mortgage as a giant lifelong burden hanging over her future. Now she viewed it differently. It became a system she could actively manage and improve rather than passively endure.

That shift changed her entire financial mindset.

She started reading books about investing, retirement planning, and wealth building. She became more conscious of interest costs in all areas of her life. Instead of focusing only on monthly affordability, she began evaluating long-term financial consequences more carefully.

Five years later, Melissa attended another retirement workshop at school. This time, the conversation about long-term debt felt completely different to her.

While many coworkers worried about carrying mortgage payments deep into retirement, Melissa realized she was years ahead of her original payoff schedule. Her accelerated payments had quietly transformed her financial trajectory.

One younger teacher approached her afterward and asked how she managed to reduce her balance so quickly on a teacher's salary.

Melissa smiled because the answer sounded almost too simple.

"I finally learned how my mortgage actually worked," she said.
Over the next several years, Melissa continued the strategy steadily. She never became obsessed or extreme. She simply remained consistent.

Eventually, her mortgage balance dropped low enough that she began seeing real freedom approaching. The possibility of living without a mortgage payment no longer felt distant or unrealistic.

By her early fifties, Melissa had reduced her mortgage dramatically ahead of schedule. She also had stronger retirement savings, lower stress levels, and greater financial confidence than she ever imagined possible during her early teaching years.

One evening she sat quietly on her back porch watching the sunset over her backyard garden. As she reviewed her latest mortgage statement, she realized something profound.

The biggest transformation had not been the money itself.

The real transformation was knowledge.

Understanding amortization changed the way she viewed debt, wealth, and financial decision-making forever. Once she understood where her mortgage money was truly going, she gained the ability to redirect her future intentionally.

And from that moment forward, every extra payment represented more than principal reduction. It represented freedom.

Chapter 3

Setting Up a Successful Biweekly Mortgage Payment System Without Costly Mistakes

One of the biggest reasons many homeowners fail to maximize the benefits of mortgage acceleration strategies is not because the strategies themselves are ineffective, but because the implementation process is often misunderstood. The biweekly mortgage payment strategy is simple in theory, yet many borrowers unknowingly make mistakes that reduce its effectiveness, create unnecessary fees, or complicate their finances unnecessarily. Understanding how to properly establish a biweekly mortgage payment system is essential for achieving long-term success.

The good news is that setting up a successful biweekly mortgage strategy does not require advanced financial expertise, expensive services, or complicated software. In fact, one of the greatest strengths of the strategy is its simplicity. However, homeowners must approach the process carefully and intentionally. A poorly structured payment system can create confusion, cash flow issues, or missed opportunities to accelerate principal reduction effectively. The first step is understanding your current mortgage structure completely. Before making any adjustments, homeowners should review their loan details carefully. This includes understanding the interest rate, loan term, monthly payment amount, escrow structure, payment due date, and whether the lender applies additional payments automatically toward principal reduction.

Many borrowers assume that every extra dollar they send automatically reduces principal, but this is not always true. Some lenders may apply additional funds differently unless borrowers specifically instruct them otherwise. In certain situations, extra money may simply be held as future payment credit rather than applied directly toward principal reduction. This mistake can significantly reduce the effectiveness of an acceleration strategy.

Homeowners should contact their mortgage servicer directly and ask clear questions regarding how additional payments are processed. Understanding the lender's procedures helps prevent confusion later. Borrowers should specifically ask whether partial biweekly payments are accepted, whether extra funds are automatically applied to principal, and whether any fees are associated with payment restructuring programs.

One of the most common mistakes homeowners make is enrolling in unnecessary third-party biweekly payment services. Many companies market mortgage acceleration programs that promise to help borrowers pay off their mortgages faster. While some services are legitimate, many charge enrollment fees, monthly maintenance fees, transaction fees, or administrative costs that reduce the financial benefit of the strategy.

Some homeowners unknowingly pay hundreds or even thousands of dollars in fees over time for services they could often replicate independently at little or no cost. In many cases, borrowers can achieve nearly identical results simply by organizing their own payment schedule and making additional principal payments directly to the lender.

This does not mean every external payment service is harmful. Some borrowers value automation assistance or convenience. However, homeowners should evaluate whether the cost of the service justifies the actual benefit provided. Financial efficiency matters because every unnecessary fee reduces wealth-building potential.

One of the simplest ways to create a biweekly structure independently is through budgeting automation. Instead of relying on an outside company, homeowners can divide their monthly mortgage payment in half and transfer that amount into a designated account every two weeks. Once enough funds accumulate, the full mortgage payment is sent to the lender according to the required due date.

In addition, borrowers can make one extra monthly payment annually by either sending additional principal manually or allowing the biweekly accumulation process to naturally create the equivalent of thirteen payments per year. This approach often gives homeowners more control and flexibility while avoiding unnecessary fees.

Cash flow management is another critical factor in building a successful system. Although the biweekly strategy feels manageable for many households, homeowners must still ensure the payment structure aligns comfortably with their income patterns and overall financial obligations. Financial acceleration should create stability rather than stress.

Some borrowers become overly aggressive too quickly. Motivated by the desire to eliminate debt rapidly, they commit to payment structures that leave little room for emergencies, repairs, medical expenses, or temporary income disruptions. While enthusiasm is valuable, sustainability is even more important.

The most successful mortgage acceleration systems are usually those that can be maintained consistently over many years. Financial systems that create constant pressure or anxiety often become difficult to sustain long term. Consistency almost always outperforms short periods of extreme intensity followed by burnout or financial setbacks.

Homeowners should also maintain healthy emergency reserves while pursuing accelerated payoff goals. A strong emergency fund provides flexibility and prevents homeowners from relying heavily on credit cards or personal loans during unexpected situations. Liquidity matters because life rarely unfolds perfectly according to plan.

Another important consideration involves budgeting psychology. One reason the biweekly strategy works so effectively is because smaller, more frequent payments often feel easier emotionally than large monthly obligations. Many people manage money better when payments align naturally with paycheck cycles.

For borrowers paid biweekly, the strategy can feel particularly seamless because it mirrors income timing. Instead of receiving a paycheck and waiting several weeks for a large mortgage payment to become due, borrowers continuously allocate smaller portions toward housing expenses throughout the month. This can reduce financial pressure and improve budgeting discipline. Automation can dramatically increase the likelihood of long-term success. Human behavior is often inconsistent, especially when emotions, stress, or busy schedules interfere with financial planning. Automatic transfers remove much of the emotional decision-making process and create consistency through systems rather than motivation alone.

Many financially successful individuals rely heavily on automation because they understand that disciplined systems often outperform willpower. By automating transfers, homeowners reduce the risk of forgetting payments, delaying extra contributions, or spending money impulsively before allocating it toward financial goals.

Technology has made mortgage acceleration easier than ever before. Most banks now allow automatic transfers, recurring payments, budgeting tools, and online mortgage tracking. Borrowers can monitor principal reduction progress in real time, which often creates additional motivation as balances decline faster than expected.

Another important element of a successful system involves tracking progress regularly. Financial goals become more motivating when progress is visible. Homeowners should periodically review mortgage statements, principal balances, and amortization projections to see how their strategy is affecting long-term outcomes. Seeing tangible progress reinforces positive behavior. Many borrowers become increasingly motivated after realizing their mortgage payoff date is moving closer year after year. Momentum creates confidence, and confidence strengthens discipline.

It is also important for homeowners to understand how additional principal payments affect future interest calculations. Every extra dollar applied toward principal reduces the balance upon which future interest is calculated. This creates compounding savings over time.

For example, even modest additional principal payments made consistently over several years may eliminate large amounts of future interest. Borrowers who fully understand this concept often become highly motivated because they realize small financial decisions today can create massive long-term results.

Another mistake homeowners sometimes make is focusing exclusively on mortgage payoff while neglecting broader financial priorities. Mortgage acceleration should exist within the context of an overall financial strategy. Retirement planning, insurance coverage, liquidity, tax planning, and investment opportunities all remain important considerations.

Some individuals may benefit from balancing mortgage acceleration with investing. Others may prioritize eliminating debt aggressively because emotional security matters more to them than maximizing theoretical investment returns. Personal finance is deeply individual, and there is no universal formula that fits every situation.

Communication between spouses or family members also plays a major role in long-term success. Financial strategies work best when everyone involved understands the goals and expectations clearly. Misalignment between partners can create stress, confusion, or inconsistent financial habits.

Families should discuss why they are pursuing mortgage acceleration and what long-term benefits they hope to achieve. Some families prioritize retiring early. Others want lower monthly obligations, increased security, investment flexibility, or the ability to help their children financially in the future. Clear goals create stronger commitment.

Another overlooked aspect of mortgage payoff systems is emotional flexibility. Life circumstances may change unexpectedly. Job transitions, business opportunities, health concerns, or economic shifts may temporarily require adjustments to financial strategies. Homeowners should avoid viewing temporary setbacks as failures.

Financial progress rarely occurs in a perfectly straight line. The key is maintaining long-term consistency despite occasional disruptions. Sustainable systems allow adaptation without completely abandoning financial goals.

As homeowners become more financially disciplined, many discover additional opportunities to accelerate progress naturally. Salary increases, side income, bonuses, rental cash flow, or reduced expenses may eventually allow larger principal reductions. What begins as a modest biweekly strategy can evolve into a powerful long-term wealth acceleration system.

One of the most empowering realizations borrowers experience is understanding that they are not trapped by the original mortgage timeline. Most people assume a thirty-year mortgage must last thirty years. In reality, homeowners have far more control than they initially realize.

Every extra principal payment changes the future. Every accelerated reduction weakens the lender's long-term interest advantage. Every disciplined financial decision shifts the balance of power slightly back toward the homeowner.

Ultimately, setting up a successful biweekly mortgage system is not about perfection. It is about creating a structure that supports steady progress, financial confidence, and long-term sustainability. Small disciplined actions repeated consistently over many years often produce extraordinary results. The homeowners who succeed with mortgage acceleration are rarely the ones with perfect circumstances. Instead, they are usually the ones who develop clear systems, maintain discipline, avoid costly mistakes, and remain committed to long-term progress. Financial freedom is often built gradually, quietly, and consistently rather than dramatically.

By understanding how to structure your biweekly strategy properly, you position yourself to reduce unnecessary interest, accelerate equity growth, and move steadily closer to a future with greater financial flexibility and peace of mind.

The Couple Who Nearly Ruined Their Finances Trying to Pay Off Their Mortgage Early

Jason and Nicole Bennett were determined to become debt-free as quickly as possible. After attending several financial seminars and watching countless online videos about financial freedom, they became obsessed with the idea of eliminating their mortgage early.

At first, their motivation came from a positive place. They wanted security for their children, lower monthly expenses, and long-term peace of mind. Jason worked in medical equipment sales, while Nicole operated a small photography business from home. Together, they earned a solid income and believed aggressive mortgage payoff would transform their future.

When they first discovered the biweekly mortgage payment strategy, they became excited immediately. The idea sounded simple and powerful. Instead of allowing the mortgage to stretch across thirty years, they imagined cutting years off the loan and saving huge amounts in interest.

However, their enthusiasm quickly turned into overconfidence.

Without fully understanding their overall cash flow, Jason and Nicole aggressively increased their mortgage payments far beyond what their budget could comfortably support. They signed up for a third-party mortgage acceleration company that promised to "eliminate the mortgage in half the time."

The company charged a large enrollment fee along with monthly administrative fees. At the time, Jason barely questioned the costs because he was so focused on becoming debt-free quickly.

"We'll save way more than the fees anyway," he told Nicole confidently.

Initially, everything felt exciting. They cut restaurant spending dramatically, canceled vacations, reduced entertainment expenses, and redirected nearly every extra dollar toward the mortgage.

For several months, they felt proud of their discipline.

Then reality began catching up with them.

Nicole's photography business experienced a slow season unexpectedly. Around the same time, Jason's company reduced commission payouts because of changes in the medical sales market. Suddenly, the aggressive mortgage payments that once felt manageable began creating serious pressure.

Their emergency savings account had also become dangerously low because they had prioritized mortgage acceleration over maintaining liquidity.

One evening, their air conditioning system failed during the middle of summer. The repair cost several thousand dollars.

Instead of paying cash comfortably, they were forced to use high-interest credit cards because most of their available funds had already been sent toward the mortgage principal.

For the first time, Nicole began questioning their strategy.

“Are we actually helping ourselves,” she asked one night, “or are we making ourselves financially fragile?”

Jason felt frustrated because he realized she had a point.

Over the next several months, additional stress emerged. Car repairs, irregular business income, and rising insurance costs created constant financial tension. Although they were technically reducing their mortgage balance faster, they were also living under increasing pressure every month.

Their obsession with rapid payoff had unintentionally weakened their financial stability.

One weekend, Jason met with an older financial advisor who specialized in retirement planning. After reviewing their situation carefully, the advisor gave them advice that surprised them.

“You’re not failing because you want to pay off your mortgage early,” he explained calmly. “You’re struggling because your system is not sustainable.”

The advisor explained that financial acceleration should strengthen stability rather than destroy it. He pointed out that while reducing mortgage debt was beneficial, maintaining liquidity and flexibility was equally important.

"You built an aggressive strategy," he said, "but you forgot to build a resilient one."

That sentence stayed with Jason for weeks.

For the first time, he realized they had approached mortgage payoff emotionally rather than strategically. They became so focused on speed that they ignored balance. The advisor then showed them how to restructure their finances more intelligently.

Instead of making extreme additional payments, he recommended returning to a manageable biweekly strategy that aligned naturally with their income. He also encouraged them to rebuild emergency savings aggressively before accelerating principal reductions further.

At first, Jason felt disappointed because slowing down felt like failure. But over time, he realized the new approach created something they had lost completely: peace.

They canceled the expensive third-party acceleration service and began handling the process themselves. They automated half-payments biweekly while maintaining stronger cash reserves. They also stopped treating every extra dollar as mandatory mortgage money.

Surprisingly, the new strategy worked much better emotionally.

Without constant financial pressure, they became more consistent. Nicole's business eventually improved, Jason's commissions stabilized, and their emergency fund began growing steadily again.

Most importantly, they no longer felt trapped by their own financial plan. Over the next several years, their mortgage balance continued shrinking faster than the original schedule, but now the process felt sustainable. They still made occasional extra principal payments during stronger income periods, but they no longer sacrificed stability to chase unrealistic timelines.

One evening, Nicole reviewed their updated amortization schedule while sitting at the kitchen table.

"We're still years ahead," she said with surprise.

Jason smiled. "Yeah. Just without the panic attacks this time."

They both laughed.

What they eventually realized was that successful mortgage payoff was not about being extreme. It was about building systems that could survive real life.

Life included slow income months, repairs, emergencies, unexpected opportunities, and changing priorities. Financial strategies needed enough flexibility to adapt without collapsing under pressure.

Years later, when friends asked Jason how they accelerated their mortgage payoff successfully, he always emphasized one lesson above everything else.

"Do it sustainably," he would say. "A strategy that works for twenty years is far more powerful than one that burns you out in six months."

By avoiding costly mistakes and learning to balance discipline with stability, Jason and Nicole eventually transformed their financial future—not through perfection, but through consistency, flexibility, and intelligent planning.

And in the end, that balance became the true foundation of their financial freedom.

Chapter 4

Creating a Long-Term Mortgage Payoff Mindset That Builds Financial Freedom

One of the greatest differences between homeowners who successfully eliminate their mortgage early and those who remain trapped in long-term debt for decades is not income, luck, or even financial intelligence alone. The true difference often comes down to mindset. Mortgage acceleration is not simply a mathematical strategy. It is a long-term behavioral system built on discipline, consistency, patience, and intentional financial thinking.

Many people begin their mortgage journey focused entirely on monthly affordability. They ask whether they can qualify for the loan, whether the payment fits their budget, and whether they can comfortably manage homeownership expenses. While these questions are important, they represent only the beginning of the financial journey. Long-term wealth is not built merely by qualifying for debt. It is built by learning how to control, reduce, and strategically manage that debt over time.

The average homeowner enters a mortgage agreement expecting to remain in debt for thirty years because that timeline feels normal. Society has conditioned people to believe that carrying a mortgage for decades is simply part of adult life. Yet the truth is that many homeowners have far more control over their mortgage timeline than they realize. Once people begin understanding how principal reduction, interest savings, and payment timing work together, their perspective often changes completely.

A mortgage payoff mindset begins with one critical realization: every financial decision has long-term consequences. Small daily spending habits, payment behaviors, and budgeting choices may seem insignificant in the moment, but over years and decades, they compound dramatically. Just as interest compounds for lenders, discipline compounds for homeowners.

This principle applies far beyond mortgages. Financial freedom is rarely achieved through one massive event alone. Instead, it is usually created through repeated intelligent decisions over long periods of time. The homeowner who consistently applies small additional amounts toward principal every year often outperforms the homeowner who waits for a perfect moment to make huge lump-sum payments that never actually occur.

Consistency matters more than perfection.

One reason many homeowners struggle financially is because modern culture constantly encourages short-term gratification. Advertisements, social media, and consumer trends pressure people to spend money immediately on lifestyle upgrades, luxury purchases, and appearances. Cars become larger, vacations become more expensive, and homes become filled with financed purchases. Meanwhile, debt quietly expands in the background.

A mortgage payoff mindset shifts this perspective entirely. Instead of focusing only on immediate comfort, homeowners begin thinking in terms of future freedom. Every extra principal payment becomes an investment in reducing future obligations. Every accelerated reduction becomes a step toward greater control over life and finances.

This does not mean homeowners must eliminate all enjoyment or live under constant deprivation. Sustainable financial progress almost never comes from extreme short-term sacrifice alone. Instead, it comes from aligning spending behavior with long-term priorities.

For example, many homeowners spend hundreds or thousands of dollars monthly on nonessential expenses without fully understanding the opportunity cost attached to those decisions. Opportunity cost refers to what that money could have accomplished elsewhere over time. A family that consistently redirects even modest amounts toward principal reduction may save tens or hundreds of thousands of dollars in interest over the life of a mortgage.

Once homeowners understand opportunity cost deeply, financial decisions begin feeling different emotionally. Small spending choices are no longer viewed only in terms of immediate pleasure. They are viewed in terms of future flexibility, reduced stress, and accelerated financial independence.

The mortgage payoff mindset also requires emotional patience. One of the biggest challenges in long-term financial improvement is that progress often feels slow in the beginning. Mortgage balances do not disappear overnight. Interest savings accumulate gradually. Equity builds steadily rather than dramatically.

This can become discouraging for people accustomed to instant results.

However, wealth-building systems are often exponential rather than linear. In the early stages, progress may appear small. Over time, momentum grows stronger and stronger. Principal reduction accelerates. Interest savings expand. Financial confidence increases. Eventually, the homeowner begins noticing major differences between their financial position and the position of people who remained passive with debt. Patience allows compounding to work.

Another critical aspect of the mortgage payoff mindset is understanding that debt reduction creates freedom, not limitation. Some people mistakenly view aggressive mortgage management as restrictive because it requires discipline. In reality, reducing long-term debt obligations often expands life choices dramatically.

A homeowner without a mortgage payment may have far greater flexibility in career decisions, retirement planning, family opportunities, business investments, or lifestyle choices. Lower fixed expenses reduce financial pressure and increase resilience during economic uncertainty.

For example, someone carrying a large mortgage payment deep into retirement may feel forced to continue working longer than desired. In contrast, someone who eliminated the mortgage earlier may experience dramatically lower monthly expenses, allowing greater freedom in how they spend their time and energy.

The psychological impact of reduced debt is also profound. Many people underestimate the stress created by long-term financial obligations. Even high-income earners often feel underlying anxiety knowing large mortgage payments must continue for decades regardless of economic conditions, employment changes, or life disruptions. Accelerating mortgage payoff reduces that psychological burden gradually over time. As balances decline faster, homeowners often experience increased confidence and peace of mind. Financial security becomes more tangible.

The mortgage payoff mindset also encourages intentional financial planning overall. Once homeowners begin focusing on debt reduction strategically, they often improve other financial habits as well. Budgeting becomes more organized. Savings increase. Spending becomes more conscious. Investments become more intentional.

Discipline spreads.

One of the most empowering realizations homeowners experience is understanding that wealth is not determined solely by income. Many high earners remain financially stressed because spending rises as income rises. Meanwhile, moderate-income households that manage debt intelligently often build substantial long-term stability and wealth.

Mortgage acceleration demonstrates this clearly. A household does not necessarily need extraordinary income to reduce debt faster. Instead, consistent discipline and intelligent systems often produce surprisingly powerful results over time. Another important mindset shift involves viewing home equity strategically. Many homeowners treat equity growth passively, assuming it will happen automatically through appreciation alone. While appreciation can certainly increase wealth, accelerated principal reduction creates guaranteed equity growth regardless of market conditions.

This stronger ownership position can provide opportunities later in life. Increased equity may support investment properties, business funding, retirement flexibility, or financial security during uncertain times. Ownership creates leverage.

At the same time, homeowners must maintain balance. The goal of mortgage payoff is not to create financial obsession or unhealthy scarcity thinking. Money should remain a tool for improving life, not a constant source of fear or guilt.

Some homeowners become so focused on eliminating debt that thcy forget to enjoy the life they are building. Financial freedom should support relationships, health, experiences, and peace of mind rather than replace them.

Balance is essential.

The most successful homeowners often create systems that allow both progress and sustainability. They automate biweekly payments, maintain emergency reserves, continue investing for retirement, and still allow room for family experiences and personal fulfillment. Financial success becomes far more sustainable when discipline and enjoyment coexist.

Long-term mortgage success also requires adaptability. Life changes constantly. Income levels shift. Expenses rise and fall. Opportunities emerge unexpectedly. A strong financial mindset allows homeowners to adjust strategies without abandoning long-term goals entirely.

There may be periods where aggressive principal reduction becomes easier because income increases. There may also be periods where maintaining liquidity temporarily becomes more important. Flexibility strengthens resilience.

Another major component of the mortgage payoff mindset is personal responsibility. Many people blame external factors entirely for their financial struggles while ignoring behaviors within their own control. Although economic conditions certainly matter, disciplined homeowners focus primarily on what they can influence directly.

They cannot control interest rate markets completely, but they can control payment habits. They cannot predict every economic cycle, but they can strengthen savings and reduce debt. They cannot eliminate uncertainty entirely, but they can increase stability through preparation.

This mindset creates empowerment rather than helplessness.

Over time, homeowners who embrace long-term financial thinking often discover something surprising. The journey itself changes them. The habits required for mortgage acceleration—discipline, patience, intentionality, consistency, and delayed gratification—begin influencing every area of financial life positively.

By the time many borrowers finally eliminate their mortgage completely, they are no longer the same people financially. Their relationship with money has matured. Their understanding of debt has evolved. Their confidence has strengthened.

And perhaps most importantly, they realize that financial freedom was never only about the house itself.

It was about reclaiming control over time, stress, opportunity, and future choices.

A mortgage payoff mindset transforms the mortgage from a passive thirty-year obligation into an active wealth-building strategy. Instead of allowing debt to quietly consume decades of future income, homeowners begin directing their finances intentionally toward long-term stability and independence.

Every extra payment becomes more than mathematics.

It becomes momentum. It becomes confidence.

It becomes freedom slowly built one disciplined decision at a time.

How a Biweekly Mortgage Strategy Saves Years and Interest

Let's look at a realistic mortgage example to fully understand how powerful the biweekly mortgage payment strategy can become over time.

Scenario

A homeowner purchases a property with the following mortgage:

- Loan Amount: $400,000
- Interest Rate: 6.75% fixed
- Loan Term: 30 years
- Monthly Principal & Interest Payment: Approximately $2,594

If the borrower follows the original monthly payment schedule for the full 30 years:

- Total Payments Over 30 Years: $2,594 × 360 months = $933,840
- Total Interest Paid: $933,840 – $400,000 = $533,840

This means the homeowner pays over half a million dollars in interest alone over the life of the mortgage.

Now let's apply the biweekly strategy.

Biweekly Payment Structure

Instead of making one monthly payment of $2,594, the borrower pays:

- $1,297 every two weeks

Because there are 52 weeks in a year:

- 26 half-payments are made annually
- 26 half-payments = 13 full payments per year

So instead of paying:

- 12 payments annually = $31,128

The borrower now pays:

- 13 payments annually = $33,722

That equals one extra monthly payment each year applied mostly toward principal reduction.

Long-Term Results

By consistently making biweekly payments:

- Mortgage payoff time may drop from 30 years to approximately 24–25 years
- Total interest savings may exceed $120,000 depending on exact loan servicing calculations

Instead of paying approximately:

- $533,840 in interest

The borrower may pay closer to:

- Around $410,000–$420,000 in interest

What This Really Means

The homeowner:

- Eliminates roughly 5–6 years of mortgage payments
- Saves well over $100,000 in interest

- Builds equity faster
- Gains financial freedom years earlier

And importantly, this was accomplished without refinancing, without huge lump-sum payments, and without radically changing lifestyle spending.

The strategy worked because of consistency and time.

Additional Perspective

If the homeowner invests the future mortgage payment after the loan is paid off early, the long-term financial impact becomes even larger.

For example:

If the homeowner continues investing the old mortgage payment of approximately $2,594 monthly for the next 5 years after early payoff into investments averaging 8% annual growth, the account could potentially grow to well over $190,000 during that period.

This demonstrates a powerful financial truth:

Reducing debt faster not only saves interest—it also creates future investing power and financial flexibility that can compound wealth even further over time.

- Builds equity faster
- Gains financial freedom years earlier

And importantly, this was accomplished without refinancing, without huge lump-sum payments, and without radically changing lifestyle spending.

The strategy worked because of consistency and time.

If the homeowner invests the future mortgage payment after the loan is paid off early, the long-term financial impact becomes even larger.

For example:

If the homeowner continues investing the old mortgage payment of approximately $2,594 monthly for the next 5 years after early payoff into investments averaging 8% annual growth, the account could potentially grow to well over $190,000 during that period.

This demonstrates a powerful financial truth:

Reducing debt faster not only saves interest—it also creates future investing power and financial flexibility that can compound wealth even further over time.

Chapter 5

Combining Biweekly Payments with Extra Principal Strategies for Maximum Acceleration

The biweekly mortgage payment strategy is powerful on its own, but when combined with additional principal reduction techniques, the results can become even more extraordinary. Many homeowners begin with biweekly payments because the strategy feels manageable and sustainable. Over time, however, they often discover that even modest additional contributions toward principal can dramatically accelerate mortgage payoff and increase long-term interest savings.

One of the most important lessons in mortgage acceleration is understanding that no single strategy exists in isolation. Financial systems become far more effective when multiple small advantages work together consistently over time. A homeowner who combines biweekly payments with periodic extra principal contributions may reduce their mortgage timeline far more aggressively than someone relying on only one method alone.

To understand why this combination works so effectively, homeowners must revisit the concept of amortization.

Mortgage interest is calculated based on the remaining principal balance. Every dollar applied directly toward principal reduces future interest calculations. The earlier those reductions occur, the greater the long-term savings often become.

Biweekly payments already create accelerated principal reduction by effectively adding one extra payment annually. However, additional lump-sum principal contributions create another layer of acceleration. These contributions can come from bonuses, tax refunds, commissions, overtime pay, business profits, side income, gifts, or reduced spending in other areas.

The true power emerges when these strategies compound together.

For example, a homeowner making biweekly payments while also applying annual tax refunds toward principal may remove years from the mortgage timeline far faster than expected. Each extra reduction weakens future interest accumulation and strengthens the impact of future payments.

One reason many homeowners underestimate the effectiveness of extra principal payments is because they focus only on the immediate balance reduction rather than the future interest eliminated. A $5,000 principal payment does far more than reduce the balance by $5,000. It also prevents years of future interest from accumulating on that portion of the debt.

This creates what can be described as "interest elimination momentum." Every principal reduction weakens the lender's future interest advantage. Over time, these reductions begin compounding against the loan structure itself.

The timing of extra payments matters tremendously. Principal reductions made early in the loan term often create much larger long-term savings than the same reductions made later. This is because early reductions affect many remaining years of future interest calculations.

For example, applying an extra $10,000 toward principal during the third year of a mortgage may save substantially more interest than applying the same amount during year twenty-five. Time amplifies the impact of early financial decisions.

Many financially disciplined homeowners intentionally design systems that capture irregular income and redirect portions toward mortgage acceleration. Instead of allowing bonuses or windfalls to disappear into lifestyle inflation, they use part of those funds strategically to reduce long-term debt.

Lifestyle inflation is one of the biggest obstacles to long-term wealth creation. As income increases, many people gradually increase spending in ways that prevent real financial progress. Larger homes, expensive vehicles, luxury purchases, and constant upgrades quietly absorb income gains that could otherwise strengthen financial stability.

Homeowners who maintain discipline during income growth periods often create extraordinary financial momentum. A raise or bonus that once would have disappeared into temporary consumption can instead shorten years of mortgage payments and save enormous amounts of future interest.

This does not mean homeowners must avoid enjoyment or live under extreme restriction. Sustainable financial acceleration works best when balance exists. The goal is not deprivation. The goal is intentionality. Every dollar should serve a purpose aligned with long-term priorities.

One effective strategy involves splitting unexpected income between enjoyment and financial progress. For example, a homeowner receiving a $10,000 bonus might allocate part toward vacation or personal enjoyment while directing the remainder toward principal reduction. This creates both lifestyle satisfaction and financial acceleration simultaneously.

Automation also becomes increasingly important as mortgage acceleration strategies expand. Many homeowners successfully automate biweekly payments while making manual principal reductions during stronger financial periods. Automation creates consistency, while manual contributions allow flexibility.

Another powerful approach involves rounding up mortgage payments regularly. For example, a borrower with a monthly payment of $2,347 may consistently pay $2,500 instead. Although the difference feels relatively small monthly, the long-term impact can become substantial over years.

Small repeated overpayments often create surprising results because of compound interest savings. Many homeowners discover that even modest consistent extra payments dramatically alter amortization schedules over time.

Some families create "mortgage freedom funds" where side income, garage sale profits, freelance work, cashback rewards, or reduced expenses are accumulated specifically for principal reduction. These systems reinforce financial focus while creating visible progress.

Another highly effective strategy involves applying raises or salary increases strategically. Many people immediately increase lifestyle spending after receiving higher income.

However, homeowners who redirect portions of raises toward mortgage acceleration often create long-term wealth much faster while still improving lifestyle gradually.

For example, if a homeowner receives a $500 monthly raise and applies $300 toward additional principal consistently, the long-term impact can become enormous. Because the household already functioned before the raise occurred, the redirected income often feels less painful emotionally.

This principle is sometimes called "capturing lifestyle drift." Instead of allowing all additional income to disappear into expanded spending, disciplined homeowners redirect part of it toward future financial freedom.

One important psychological advantage of combining strategies is increased motivation. Visible progress creates momentum. As homeowners see balances shrinking faster, they often become increasingly disciplined and financially aware overall.

Mortgage acceleration frequently becomes a gateway toward broader financial transformation. Many homeowners who begin with biweekly payments eventually improve budgeting habits, eliminate consumer debt, strengthen emergency savings, increase investments, and become more intentional with money overall.

Financial confidence grows through action.

Another major benefit of accelerated principal reduction is increased equity growth. Faster equity accumulation improves financial flexibility and resilience. Homeowners with stronger equity positions may qualify for better refinancing options, investment opportunities, or improved borrowing terms if needed in the future.

Increased equity can also create emotional security during economic uncertainty. During housing downturns or job instability, homeowners with lower balances and stronger ownership positions often experience less stress than heavily leveraged borrowers.

However, homeowners must avoid becoming overly aggressive to the point of creating financial vulnerability. Mortgage acceleration should strengthen stability rather than weaken liquidity. Emergency reserves remain essential because unexpected expenses are inevitable.

Some homeowners make the mistake of sending every available dollar toward principal while neglecting savings entirely. This can create serious problems during emergencies, medical situations, business disruptions, or major repairs. Financial flexibility matters.

The most successful long-term strategies usually balance debt reduction with liquidity and investment growth. Homeowners should create systems that support both acceleration and resilience.

Another important consideration is tax efficiency and investment opportunity cost. Depending on interest rates and potential investment returns, some borrowers may choose to balance mortgage acceleration with investing in retirement accounts, businesses, or appreciating assets.

There is no universal formula that fits every homeowner. Some people value emotional peace and debt elimination above maximizing theoretical investment returns. Others prioritize investing excess cash while maintaining low-interest mortgage debt. Personal goals matter.

Still, understanding how extra principal affects mortgage payoff empowers homeowners to make informed decisions intentionally rather than passively following default structures.

Technology makes this easier than ever before. Mortgage calculators, budgeting apps, and amortization tools allow borrowers to model countless scenarios instantly. Homeowners can see exactly how additional principal payments affect payoff dates and interest savings.

These tools often create major mindset shifts. Once borrowers visually see how small additional contributions eliminate years of debt, motivation increases dramatically. One overlooked aspect of mortgage acceleration is the emotional satisfaction associated with progress itself. Many homeowners feel trapped by long-term debt because they believe they have little control over the timeline. Accelerated payoff strategies restore a sense of agency.

Every extra payment becomes proof that progress is possible.

Over time, homeowners often discover that financial freedom is built gradually through systems rather than dramatic one-time events. The combination of biweekly payments and extra principal reduction creates a powerful example of this principle.

Small disciplined actions repeated consistently over many years create results that initially seem impossible.

A homeowner does not necessarily need massive wealth to reduce a mortgage significantly faster. Instead, they need awareness, intentionality, patience, and systems capable of compounding over time.

This realization is empowering because it shifts focus away from external circumstances and toward controllable behaviors. Financial transformation becomes less about luck and more about consistency.

Ultimately, combining biweekly payments with extra principal strategies creates a highly effective framework for reducing interest, accelerating equity growth, and increasing long-term financial flexibility. The process may begin slowly, but momentum compounds steadily.

Every additional principal payment shortens the future.

Every interest dollar avoided strengthens future wealth.

And every disciplined financial decision moves the homeowner closer to a life with greater freedom, opportunity, and peace of mind.

Combining Biweekly Payments and Extra Principal to Eliminate a Mortgage Over 10 Years Early

Let's look at a realistic mortgage scenario showing how combining biweekly payments with extra principal contributions can dramatically reduce both payoff time and total interest paid.

Original Mortgage Scenario

A homeowner purchases a property with the following loan:

- Loan Amount: $500,000

- Interest Rate: 6.5% fixed

- Loan Term: 30 years

- Monthly Principal & Interest Payment: Approximately $3,160

Standard 30-Year Mortgage Outcome

If the borrower simply follows the standard payment schedule:

- Monthly Payment: $3,160

- Total Payments Over 30 Years: $3,160 × 360 = $1,137,600

- Total Interest Paid: $1,137,600 – $500,000 = $637,600

This means the borrower pays over $637,000 in interest over the life of the loan.

Now let's apply a combined acceleration strategy.

Step 1: Convert to Biweekly Payments

Instead of making one monthly payment of $3,160, the borrower pays:

- $1,580 every two weeks

Because there are 26 biweekly periods annually:

- 26 half-payments = 13 full payments annually

This creates the equivalent of one extra full payment every year.

Estimated Impact of Biweekly Payments Alone

Approximate results:

- Mortgage payoff reduced from 30 years to about 25 years
- Interest savings may exceed $120,000–$140,000 depending on exact amortization calculations

But now we add another layer.

Step 2: Add Extra Principal Payments

The homeowner also applies:

- $5,000 annual tax refund toward principal
- $300 extra principal monthly from side income

Additional Annual Principal Reduction

- Monthly extra payments: $300 × 12 = $3,600 annually

- Tax refund applied annually: $5,000
- Total extra principal annually: $8,600

Combined with the extra annual biweekly payment:

- Additional mortgage acceleration becomes extremely powerful.

Estimated Combined Results

With:

- Biweekly payments
- $300 extra monthly principal
- $5,000 annual lump-sum payment

The borrower may achieve:

- Mortgage payoff in approximately 18–19 years instead of 30 years
- Total interest savings potentially exceeding $300,000

Instead of paying:

- Approximately $637,600 in total interest

The borrower may pay closer to:

- Around $320,000–$340,000 in total interest

Financial Impact

Years Eliminated

- Roughly 11–12 years removed from the mortgage timeline

Interest Saved

- Approximately $300,000+ saved

Equity Growth

The homeowner builds equity dramatically faster because principal reduction accelerates early in the loan.

What Happens After Mortgage Payoff?

Now imagine the borrower continues investing the old mortgage payment after the loan is eliminated early.

If they invest:

- $3,160 monthly
- For the next 10 years
- At an average 8% annual investment return

The investment account could potentially grow to well over:

- $580,000–$600,000+

This demonstrates an important principle:

Mortgage acceleration does not only reduce debt. It also creates future investing power because cash flow eventually becomes available for wealth-building rather than interest payments.

Long-Term Wealth Perspective

By combining:

- Biweekly payments
- Extra monthly principal
- Annual lump-sum reductions
- Long-term investing after payoff

The homeowner potentially transforms:

- Hundreds of thousands of dollars previously lost to interest

Into:

- Future investments, retirement wealth, financial security, and freedom.

Chapter 6

Avoiding Common Mortgage Payoff Mistakes That Can Slow Your Financial Progress

Paying off a mortgage early can be one of the most powerful financial achievements a homeowner ever accomplishes. It can reduce stress, eliminate years of debt, save massive amounts of interest, and create long-term financial flexibility. However, while many homeowners begin mortgage acceleration plans with excitement and motivation, not everyone achieves the results they originally envisioned. In many cases, the problem is not the strategy itself. The problem is avoidable mistakes that quietly slow progress, reduce efficiency, or create financial instability along the way.

Understanding these mistakes is critical because even strong financial habits can becomc less effective when paired with poor planning or emotional decision-making. Mortgage acceleration should strengthen a homeowner's financial life overall, not create unnecessary pressure, imbalance, or hidden setbacks. By recognizing common mistakes early, homeowners can build systems that are sustainable, efficient, and aligned with long-term financial freedom. One of the most common mistakes homeowners make is focusing entirely on mortgage payoff while neglecting emergency savings. Enthusiasm about becoming debt-free can sometimes cause borrowers to send every available dollar toward principal reduction while leaving little cash available for unexpected situations. Although reducing debt is valuable, financial stability requires liquidity as well.

Life is unpredictable. Medical expenses, job interruptions, vehicle repairs, home maintenance, business slowdowns, and economic downturns can occur unexpectedly. Homeowners without emergency reserves may eventually be forced to rely on high-interest credit cards, personal loans, or retirement withdrawals during emergencies. In these situations, the financial damage created by lack of liquidity may outweigh some of the benefits gained through accelerated mortgage payoff.

A strong financial foundation usually includes both debt reduction and emergency preparedness. Homeowners should aim to maintain sufficient reserves while accelerating their mortgage rather than sacrificing all flexibility in pursuit of speed. Sustainable progress almost always outperforms extreme short-term efforts that create vulnerability. Another major mistake is failing to specify that extra payments should be applied directly toward principal. Many borrowers assume additional money automatically reduces the loan balance immediately, but some lenders process extra funds differently unless specific instructions are provided. In certain cases, lenders may hold additional funds as future payment credits rather than applying them toward principal reduction.

This mistake can significantly weaken the effectiveness of mortgage acceleration strategies. Homeowners should verify how their lender handles additional payments and review statements regularly to confirm that extra amounts are reducing principal properly. Financial awareness matters because small misunderstandings can create major long-term consequences.

A third common mistake involves repeatedly refinancing into new long-term loans without understanding how amortization resets. Refinancing can absolutely be a valuable financial tool when used strategically. Lower interest rates, improved terms, or reduced monthly obligations may create substantial benefits. However, some homeowners refinance multiple times into new thirty-year loans, unintentionally restarting the interest-heavy early years of amortization again and again.

For example, a borrower who refinances every few years into a new thirty-year mortgage may spend decades primarily paying interest despite years of prior payments. Without careful analysis, refinancing can quietly extend debt timelines much longer than expected.

This does not mean refinancing should be avoided entirely. Instead, homeowners should evaluate refinancing decisions carefully within the context of long-term goals. In some cases, choosing shorter loan terms or continuing accelerated payments after refinancing may preserve the benefits while still reducing interest rates.

Another mistake homeowners often make is becoming emotionally discouraged by slow early progress. Mortgage acceleration is a long-term process, and the effects of amortization mean that balance reductions may initially feel modest. Some borrowers lose motivation because they expect dramatic visible results too quickly.

This mindset can become dangerous because consistency is what creates long-term transformation. Financial systems often produce exponential rather than immediate results. Early stages require patience. Over time, momentum builds stronger and stronger as principal reduction accelerates and interest decreases.

Homeowners who remain disciplined through the early years often experience major long-term rewards later. Those who abandon the process prematurely frequently miss the compounding effects that create extraordinary results.

Another major obstacle to mortgage acceleration is lifestyle inflation. Lifestyle inflation occurs when spending increases automatically alongside income growth. Many people receive raises, bonuses, commissions, or business growth over time, yet their financial position improves very little because expenses rise equally fast.

Larger vehicles, luxury purchases, expensive vacations, upgraded homes, and subscription-based lifestyles quietly absorb additional income that could otherwise strengthen financial freedom. Homeowners who control lifestyle inflation strategically often create enormous long-term wealth advantages because they redirect portions of income growth toward principal reduction, investing, or savings.

This does not mean homeowners should never enjoy increased income. The goal is balance and intentionality. Financial progress becomes far more powerful when income increases are used strategically rather than consumed automatically.

Another common mistake involves ignoring opportunity cost entirely. While aggressive mortgage payoff can provide tremendous emotional and financial benefits, homeowners should still evaluate broader financial priorities carefully. Retirement contributions, employer matches, business investments, insurance coverage, and tax-advantaged accounts may also deserve attention.

For example, a homeowner aggressively paying down a low-interest mortgage while neglecting retirement contributions that include employer matching may unintentionally miss valuable long-term wealth opportunities. Financial planning works best when all areas of personal finance are considered together rather than in isolation.

Some homeowners also underestimate maintenance and repair costs associated with homeownership itself. In pursuit of rapid mortgage payoff, they may neglect setting aside funds for inevitable repairs such as roofing, plumbing, appliances, air conditioning systems, or structural maintenance.

A paid-off home that requires major repairs without available savings can still create significant financial stress. Responsible homeowners balance debt reduction with ongoing property maintenance planning.

Another psychological mistake occurs when homeowners compare their financial progress constantly to others. Social comparison can distort financial decision-making. Some people feel pressured to maintain appearances or lifestyle standards that conflict with long-term financial goals. Mortgage acceleration often requires delayed gratification and intentional spending. This may look different from the behaviors of friends, coworkers, or neighbors focused primarily on consumption and visible lifestyle upgrades. Homeowners committed to long-term freedom must often resist short-term comparison pressure.

The reality is that many people appearing financially successful externally may actually be carrying enormous debt burdens privately. Appearances rarely reveal true financial stability.

Another dangerous mistake involves treating mortgage acceleration as purely emotional while ignoring mathematics completely. Some homeowners become so emotionally driven to eliminate debt that they sacrifice all investing, liquidity, or business opportunities even when their mortgage interest rate is relatively low compared to potential long-term investment returns.

On the other hand, some people focus only on maximizing theoretical investment returns while ignoring the emotional security and cash flow benefits created by debt reduction. Balance matters because personal finance involves both mathematical efficiency and human psychology.

The best strategy is often the onc homeowners can follow consistently while maintaining emotional peace and financial resilience over decades. Some borrowers also make the mistake of relying too heavily on future income assumptions. They assume raises, business growth, or future earnings will solve all financial problems later. While optimism can be healthy, long-term financial plans should remain grounded in realistic current cash flow and disciplined behavior rather than uncertain future projections.

Financial security is built strongest on stable habits rather than hopeful assumptions.

Another common issue involves lack of automation. Human behavior is inconsistent. Motivation changes. Life becomes busy. Without systems in place, homeowners may skip extra payments, delay contributions, or lose focus over time.

Automation creates consistency by reducing emotional decision-making. Automatic biweekly payments, recurring transfers, and structured budgeting systems help ensure long-term progress continues even during stressful or busy periods.

One of the most overlooked mistakes is failing to celebrate progress. Mortgage acceleration is a long journey. If homeowners focus only on the final payoff date without recognizing intermediate milestones, the process can begin feeling exhausting rather than empowering.

Celebrating milestones strengthens motivation. Watching balances decline, tracking interest savings, or recognizing years eliminated from the mortgage timeline can reinforce positive financial behavior and maintain momentum.

Another important lesson homeowners eventually learn is that financial freedom is not built through one perfect decision alone. It is built through thousands of small decisions repeated consistently over many years. The cumulative effect of discipline matters more than occasional dramatic financial moves.

Mortgage acceleration succeeds when homeowners remain patient, balanced, flexible, and intentional. Mistakes become dangerous only when they continue unnoticed for years without correction. Awareness creates opportunity for improvement.

The goal is not perfection.

The goal is progress.

Every extra principal payment still moves the homeowner forward. Every disciplined financial choice still weakens long-term interest accumulation. Every avoided mistake strengthens future stability.

Ultimately, mortgage payoff should support a larger vision of financial freedom rather than become an isolated obsession. A truly successful strategy creates reduced stress, increased flexibility, stronger savings, and greater confidence—not constant pressure and financial fragility.

Homeowners who avoid common mistakes while remaining consistent with disciplined acceleration strategies often discover something powerful over time: financial freedom is less about income level and more about intentional behavior repeated patiently over years.

And those behaviors, once developed, often transform far more than just the mortgage itself.

How Small Mortgage Mistakes Can Cost Hundreds of Thousands Over Time

Let's compare two homeowners with nearly identical financial situations to understand how small decisions and common mistakes dramatically affect long-term mortgage outcomes.

Scenario

Both homeowners purchase a property using the following mortgage:

- Loan Amount: $450,000
- Interest Rate: 6.75% fixed

- Loan Term: 30 years
- Monthly Principal & Interest Payment: Approximately $2,918

If both borrowers follow the standard 30-year schedule:

- Total Payments Over 30 Years: $2,918 × 360 = $1,050,480
- Total Interest Paid: $1,050,480 – $450,000 = $600,480

Now let's compare two different approaches.

Homeowner A — Strategic Mortgage Acceleration

This homeowner:

- Uses biweekly payments
- Adds $250 extra principal monthly
- Applies a $4,000 annual tax refund toward principal
- Maintains a healthy emergency fund
- Avoids lifestyle inflation after raises
- Continues retirement investing simultaneously

Annual Additional Principal

- Extra monthly principal: $250 × 12 = $3,000 annually
- Annual tax refund contribution: $4,000
- Additional biweekly payment effect: Approximately one extra mortgage payment annually = $2,918

Total Extra Annual Principal

Approximately:

- $9,918 annually toward acceleration

Estimated Results for Homeowner A

Approximate mortgage payoff timeline:

- Around 19–20 years instead of 30 years

Estimated total interest paid:

- Approximately $340,000–$360,000

Interest Savings

Compared to the original schedule:

- Potential savings of roughly $240,000–$260,000 in interest

Additional Benefit

Because the mortgage is eliminated roughly 10 years early, the homeowner now has an extra:

- $2,918 monthly cash flow available for investing or retirement.

Homeowner B — Common Financial Mistakes

This homeowner:

- Makes only standard monthly payments
- Frequently refinances into new 30-year loans
- Uses bonuses for lifestyle upgrades instead of principal reduction
- Carries credit card debt during emergencies due to weak savings
- Misses several opportunities for extra principal contributions
- Increases spending significantly after raises

Additional Hidden Cost

Over time:

- Credit card interest during emergencies adds approximately $25,000 extra debt costs
- Repeated refinancing resets amortization and adds closing costs totaling roughly $18,000
- No accelerated principal reduction means full long-term interest accumulation continues

Estimated Results for Homeowner B

Mortgage payoff timeline:

- Still close to full 30 years or longer due to refinancing resets

Estimated total mortgage interest:

- Approximately $600,000+

Additional refinancing and consumer debt costs:

- Approximately $40,000+ extra

Total Long-Term Cost Difference

Compared to Homeowner A:

Homeowner B may spend:

- Over $280,000–$320,000 more overall across mortgage interest, refinancing costs, and consumer debt interest.

Long-Term Wealth Difference

Now imagine Homeowner A invests the old mortgage payment after payoff:

- $2,918 monthly invested
- For 10 years after early payoff
- At an average 8% annual return

Potential investment growth:

- Approximately $530,000–$600,000+

This means the gap between the two homeowners may eventually exceed:

- $800,000+ in long-term financial difference

Even though they originally started with:

- The same mortgage
- Similar income

- Similar homes

The Key Lesson

Small financial behaviors repeated consistently over decades create enormous long-term outcomes.

Avoiding common mortgage mistakes does not merely save money.

It can completely transform a family's future wealth, flexibility, retirement options, and financial security.

Chapter 7

Using Income Growth and Cash Flow Increases to Accelerate Mortgage Freedom

One of the most powerful opportunities homeowners often overlook in the journey toward mortgage freedom is the strategic use of income growth. Many people focus entirely on reducing expenses or making small additional payments while ignoring the enormous long-term impact that increasing cash flow can have on mortgage acceleration. In reality, income growth combined with disciplined financial management can transform an ordinary mortgage payoff strategy into a highly effective wealth-building system.

Most homeowners experience some form of income increase over the course of a thirty-year mortgage. Salaries rise, businesses expand, commissions improve, side income develops, and career opportunities evolve over time. Yet despite earning more money, many households remain financially stressed because spending rises just as quickly as income. This pattern, commonly known as lifestyle inflation, quietly prevents many people from building lasting wealth. The mortgage payoff mindset requires homeowners to think differently about income growth. Instead of automatically converting every raise or financial improvement into higher spending, disciplined homeowners intentionally redirect portions of increased cash flow toward long-term financial goals. Mortgage acceleration becomes one of the most powerful uses of this additional income because of the compounding effect it creates over time.

The key concept is simple: every increase in cash flow creates a decision point. Homeowners can either consume the additional income immediately through lifestyle expansion, or they can strategically use part of it to reduce future financial obligations. While occasional lifestyle improvements are perfectly reasonable, consistently directing some income growth toward mortgage reduction can dramatically shorten the debt timeline and save extraordinary amounts in interest.

For example, imagine a homeowner receives a $600 monthly raise after taxes. Many people would gradually absorb the entire increase through upgraded spending habits without significantly improving their long-term financial position. However, a homeowner who redirects even half of that raise toward extra principal payments may eliminate years from the mortgage while still enjoying increased disposable income.

This strategy works because mortgage acceleration compounds over time. Every extra principal payment reduces future interest calculations. As interest decreases, more of each future payment goes toward principal reduction, creating accelerating momentum. The earlier income increases are applied strategically, the stronger the long-term impact becomes.

One reason this approach works so effectively psychologically is because homeowners are not necessarily sacrificing their existing lifestyle. Since the household already functioned before the raise occurred, redirecting part of the new income often feels less emotionally difficult than cutting current spending dramatically.

This creates a highly sustainable form of financial progress.

Many financially successful homeowners use what can be called the "split-growth method." Whenever income increases, they divide the additional cash flow strategically between lifestyle improvement, investing, savings, and debt reduction. This balanced approach allows continued enjoyment of life while still accelerating financial freedom.

For instance, a homeowner receiving an additional $1,000 monthly after a promotion might allocate:

- $300 toward lifestyle improvement
- $300 toward retirement investing
- $400 toward mortgage acceleration

Over time, this balanced allocation strategy can create extraordinary financial progress without creating feelings of deprivation.

Side income can become another major accelerator. In modern economies, opportunities for additional income are more accessible than ever before. Freelancing, consulting, online businesses, rental income, seasonal work, digital products, commissions, tutoring, coaching, and gig economy opportunities all provide potential cash flow streams that can strengthen mortgage payoff systems significantly.

One important distinction is that side income often feels psychologically different from primary salary income. Many homeowners find it easier to apply side earnings toward mortgage reduction because the money feels "extra" rather than necessary for core living expenses.

For example, a homeowner earning an additional $1,500 monthly from freelance work may choose to apply the majority toward principal reduction while maintaining normal living expenses from primary income. Even modest side income applied consistently can eliminate years of mortgage debt over time. Rental income also plays a powerful role in mortgage acceleration for many homeowners. House hacking, accessory dwelling units, room rentals, vacation rentals, or investment properties can generate cash flow that dramatically strengthens debt reduction capacity. In some situations, rental income alone may cover large portions of the mortgage obligation.

The concept becomes especially powerful when homeowners avoid immediately inflating their lifestyle after creating additional income streams. Many people generate higher earnings only to increase obligations proportionally through larger homes, luxury vehicles, expensive subscriptions, or consumer debt. The financial advantage disappears because spending expands as quickly as income.

Disciplined homeowners approach income growth differently. They recognize that every increase in cash flow creates leverage. Properly managed, that leverage can shorten years of debt and dramatically improve long-term financial flexibility.

Another important factor involves tax refunds and irregular income events. Many households receive periodic lump sums throughout the year through bonuses, commissions, profit distributions, or refunds. These moments create powerful opportunities for principal reduction because even occasional lump-sum payments can significantly disrupt amortization schedules. A $5,000 or $10,000 principal reduction may appear relatively small compared to a large mortgage balance, but the long-term interest savings can become surprisingly substantial when applied early in the loan term.

The timing of additional payments matters tremendously. Early reductions create larger savings because they affect future interest calculations across many remaining years of the mortgage. Homeowners who begin redirecting income strategically during the first decade of a mortgage often experience the strongest acceleration effects.

However, homeowners should avoid the mistake of becoming overly aggressive without maintaining financial stability. Income growth should strengthen resilience rather than create vulnerability. Emergency reserves, insurance protection, retirement planning, and liquidity remain essential.

Some homeowners make the mistake of assuming higher income automatically guarantees financial success. In reality, unmanaged income growth often leads to equally rapid spending growth. Wealth is not determined solely by earnings. It is determined by how effectively cash flow is managed over time.

This is why many moderate-income households eventually outperform higher-income households financially. Disciplined cash flow management matters more than appearances or temporary lifestyle upgrades.

Another important concept is fixed expense reduction. Every mortgage payment eliminated early permanently lowers required monthly obligations. This creates future flexibility that compounds long after the loan itself disappears.

For example, eliminating a $3,500 monthly mortgage payment effectively creates $42,000 annually in freed cash flow. That flexibility may eventually support early retirement, business ownership, reduced work hours, investment opportunities, travel, family support, or increased peace of mind.

Income growth strategies become even more powerful when combined with biweekly payment systems. Biweekly payments already create accelerated principal reduction through the equivalent of one extra payment annually. Additional cash flow layered on top of this structure creates even stronger momentum.

Technology has also made cash flow management easier than ever before. Budgeting tools, automatic transfers, investment apps, and online mortgage calculators allow homeowners to model scenarios instantly and automate disciplined financial behavior.

Many homeowners become deeply motivated once they visually see how additional income affects mortgage timelines. A raise that once seemed relatively insignificant suddenly becomes a tool capable of eliminating years of debt when applied consistently.

This creates an important psychological shift. Homeowners begin viewing income growth not merely as permission to spend more, but as an opportunity to create freedom faster.

The emotional impact of accelerated mortgage progress can become profound. As balances decline faster, homeowners often feel increasing confidence and security. Debt becomes less intimidating. Financial options expand. Long-term goals begin feeling realistic rather than distant.

Some homeowners eventually discover that the greatest reward is not merely becoming debt-free, but the transformation in mindset that occurs during the process. Learning to manage increasing income intentionally often strengthens every area of personal finance simultaneously.

Retirement contributions improve. Investments grow. Consumer debt declines. Savings habits strengthen. Financial stress decreases.

Mortgage acceleration through income growth becomes more than a strategy. It becomes a lifestyle built around intentionality and long-term thinking. Another overlooked benefit is increased resilience during economic uncertainty. Homeowners who reduce debt aggressively while maintaining healthy cash flow systems often experience less stress during recessions, layoffs, or market volatility because their fixed obligations decline steadily over time.

Lower required monthly expenses create freedom.

Freedom creates options.

Options create confidence.

And confidence strengthens long-term financial decision-making.

Ultimately, income growth represents one of the greatest hidden opportunities in mortgage payoff strategies. Most homeowners will earn more money throughout their lives than they initially realize. The critical question is whether those increases will quietly disappear into consumption or become tools for wealth acceleration.

Every raise, bonus, commission, or side income stream carries potential energy.

Used intentionally, that energy can eliminate years of debt, save enormous amounts in interest, and create a future with dramatically greater flexibility and peace of mind. The homeowners who achieve extraordinary financial freedom are often not those with perfect circumstances or unlimited income.

They are the ones who consistently direct growing cash flow toward long-term ownership, stability, and opportunity.

And over time, those decisions change everything.

How Redirecting Income Growth Can Eliminate a Mortgage Nearly 15 Years Early

Let's look at a realistic example showing how disciplined use of income growth and cash flow increases can dramatically accelerate mortgage payoff and long-term wealth creation.

Original Mortgage Scenario

A homeowner purchases a property with the following loan:

- Loan Amount: $550,000
- Interest Rate: 6.75% fixed

- Loan Term: 30 years
- Monthly Principal & Interest Payment: Approximately $3,567

Standard Mortgage Outcome

If the borrower follows the standard payment schedule:

- Total Payments Over 30 Years: $3,567 × 360 = $1,284,120
- Total Interest Paid: $1,284,120 – $550,000 = $734,120

This means the homeowner pays over $734,000 in interest alone if the mortgage runs the full 30 years.

Income Growth Strategy

Now imagine the homeowner follows these strategies:

Step 1 — Biweekly Payments

The homeowner converts to biweekly payments:

- $1,783.50 every two weeks

This creates the equivalent of:

- 13 full payments annually instead of 12.

Step 2 — Redirect Part of Raises

The homeowner receives:

- An average after-tax raise of $500 monthly every 3 years.

Instead of spending all of it, they redirect:

- $300 monthly toward extra principal.

Step 3 — Side Income

The homeowner earns:

- $800 monthly average side income from freelancing and consulting.

They apply:

- $500 monthly toward mortgage principal.

Step 4 — Annual Bonus

Each year the homeowner applies:

- A $6,000 work bonus toward principal reduction.

Total Additional Annual Principal

Biweekly Extra Payment Effect

Approximately:

- $3,567 annually

Extra Monthly Principal from Raises

- $300 × 12 = $3,600 annually

Side Income Contributions

- $500 × 12 = $6,000 annually

Annual Bonus

- $6,000 annually

Total Additional Principal Per Year

Approximately:

- $19,167 annually beyond the regular mortgage schedule.

Estimated Mortgage Results

Instead of:

- 30 years of payments

The homeowner may eliminate the mortgage in approximately:

- 15–16 years

Years Eliminated

- Roughly 14–15 years removed from the mortgage timeline.

Interest Savings

Instead of paying:

- Approximately $734,120 in interest

The homeowner may pay closer to:

- Around $290,000–$340,000 in total interest

Estimated Interest Saved

Approximately:

- $400,000+ saved in interest

Additional Long-Term Wealth Impact

Now imagine the homeowner continues investing the old mortgage payment after payoff.

If they invest:

- $3,567 monthly
- For the next 15 years
- At an average 8% annual return

Potential investment growth could exceed:

- $1.2 million–$1.4 million+

The Bigger Financial Lesson

The homeowner did not accomplish this through:

- Winning the lottery
- Receiving inheritance wealth
- Becoming ultra-rich overnight

Instead, they used:

- Income growth strategically
- Controlled lifestyle inflation
- Biweekly payments
- Side income

- Consistent principal reduction

The result was not only a paid-off home years earlier, but potentially millions of dollars in long-term financial difference between interest avoided and future investments created.

This demonstrates a powerful truth:

Increasing income alone does not create wealth.

Intentionally directing growing cash flow toward ownership, reduced debt, and future investing is what creates true long-term financial freedom.

Chapter 8

How to Stay Motivated During the Long Mortgage Payoff Journey

One of the greatest challenges homeowners face when pursuing early mortgage payoff is not understanding the strategy itself. The mathematics behind biweekly payments, extra principal reductions, and interest savings are relatively straightforward once properly explained. The true challenge is maintaining motivation over many years. Mortgage acceleration is not a short-term project. It is a long-term commitment that requires consistency, patience, discipline, and emotional resilience.

Many homeowners begin their payoff journey highly motivated. They calculate potential interest savings, visualize becoming debt-free years earlier, and feel excited about the possibilities ahead. In the beginning, every extra payment feels meaningful and empowering. However, as months turn into years, maintaining the same level of emotional energy becomes more difficult.

This is completely normal.

Long-term financial transformation rarely happens through constant excitement alone. Motivation naturally rises and falls over time. The homeowners who ultimately succeed are usually not the ones who remain emotionally energized every single day. Instead, they are the ones who learn how to build systems, habits, and perspectives that continue functioning even when motivation temporarily weakens.

One of the biggest psychological obstacles in mortgage payoff is the slow pace of progress during the early years. Mortgage balances often decline gradually at first because interest still consumes a large portion of each payment. Homeowners may make payments consistently for years yet feel frustrated by how much debt remains.

This frustration can become dangerous because human beings naturally crave visible results. Modern culture reinforces this expectation constantly. People are accustomed to instant communication, rapid delivery, immediate entertainment, and quick feedback. Mortgage acceleration operates differently. Its rewards are delayed and cumulative.

The key is understanding that mortgage payoff is a compounding process. Early progress often appears modest because the system is still building momentum. Over time, however, principal reduction accelerates. Interest declines. Equity grows faster. Eventually, homeowners begin seeing major differences compared to the original amortization schedule. Patience allows compounding to work.

One of the most effective ways to maintain motivation is by tracking progress visually. Many homeowners feel more encouraged when they can clearly see how extra payments are affecting their balance and payoff timeline. Mortgage calculators, amortization charts, payoff trackers, and budgeting apps can transform abstract financial goals into visible progress.

For example, instead of focusing only on the remaining balance, homeowners may track:

- Years removed from the mortgage
- Interest dollars saved
- Principal reduced annually
- Equity milestones reached
- Percentage of ownership achieved

These smaller milestones create emotional reinforcement throughout the journey.

Celebrating progress is extremely important. Too many homeowners focus exclusively on the final payoff date without recognizing intermediate victories along the way. Financial transformation is built through thousands of small disciplined decisions repeated consistently over time. Acknowledging progress strengthens confidence and reinforces positive behavior.

Some families create visual charts or "mortgage freedom countdowns" displayed in their homes. Others celebrate every major reduction milestone with simple family experiences or meaningful rewards. The goal is not excessive spending. The goal is emotional reinforcement.

Another important factor in long-term motivation is remembering why the journey began in the first place. Mortgage acceleration is rarely only about numbers. Behind the financial goals are deeper emotional motivations:

- Reduced stress
- Family security
- Early retirement
- Financial independence
- More freedom with time
- Greater peace of mind

- Ownership and stability

When homeowners reconnect emotionally with these larger goals, discipline becomes easier to sustain.

Purpose strengthens persistence.

One of the biggest threats to motivation is comparison. Social comparison can quietly destroy financial focus because it encourages homeowners to prioritize appearances over long-term freedom. Friends, coworkers, neighbors, and social media often create pressure to upgrade lifestyles constantly.

Larger homes, luxury cars, expensive vacations, designer purchases, and visible consumption may appear attractive temporarily. However, many people financing these lifestyles are also carrying enormous debt burdens privately. Appearances rarely reveal true financial stability.

Homeowners pursuing mortgage freedom must often develop the ability to resist external pressure and remain focused on long-term goals. This does not mean avoiding enjoyment or living with scarcity. It means understanding the difference between intentional spending and unconscious lifestyle inflation.

Financial confidence grows when homeowners stop measuring success by appearances and begin measuring it by flexibility, stability, and freedom. Another major challenge during long-term mortgage payoff is dealing with unexpected setbacks. Life rarely follows a perfect financial plan. Job changes, medical issues, repairs, economic downturns, family emergencies, business disruptions, and market volatility can temporarily interrupt acceleration progress.

Some homeowners become discouraged during these periods and abandon their payoff strategy entirely because they feel they are "falling behind." In reality, temporary setbacks are normal. Financial journeys are rarely linear.

The homeowners who succeed long term are usually the ones who learn flexibility. They understand that slowing down temporarily is not failure. Progress may pause at times, but disciplined systems can always resume later.

Consistency over decades matters far more than perfection over a few months.

Another important psychological strategy is automation. Relying entirely on emotional motivation can become exhausting over long periods. Automated systems reduce the need for constant willpower by turning financial discipline into routine behavior.

Automatic biweekly payments, recurring principal

contributions, and scheduled transfers help ensure progress continues even during stressful or busy seasons of life. Systems outperform emotions over time.

Many financially successful individuals rely heavily on automation because they understand human behavior fluctuates naturally. Removing unnecessary decision-making reduces friction and increases consistency.

Homeowners should also avoid becoming so obsessed with mortgage payoff that they eliminate all enjoyment from life. Financial acceleration works best when it supports overall well-being rather than creating constant deprivation. Sustainable systems allow room for family experiences, health, relationships, hobbies, and balance.

Extreme restriction often leads to burnout.

The most successful long-term mortgage strategies usually combine discipline with sustainability. Homeowners who allow themselves occasional enjoyment while remaining consistent with their larger goals often stay motivated much longer than those pursuing perfection aggressively.

Mindset also plays a critical role. Many people view debt reduction as punishment or sacrifice. Successful homeowners often reframe the process differently. Instead of focusing on what they are "giving up," they focus on what they are building:

- Future flexibility
- Lower stress
- Increased security
- Greater cash flow
- More ownership
- Freedom from obligation

This shift changes the emotional experience entirely.

Another highly effective motivational tool involves imagining life after the mortgage is gone. Many homeowners spend decades assuming mortgage payments will always exist. They rarely visualize the enormous cash flow flexibility that arrives once the payment disappears completely.

For example, eliminating a $3,500 monthly mortgage payment creates:

- $42,000 annually in freed cash flow

That money can eventually support:

- Retirement
- Travel
- Investments
- Business opportunities
- Family support
- Reduced work hours
- Financial security

Visualizing that future can make present discipline feel much more meaningful.

Another important lesson is understanding that motivation often follows action rather than preceding it. Many people wait until they "feel motivated" before making disciplined financial decisions. In reality, consistent action frequently creates motivation over time.

As homeowners watch balances decline and progress accumulate, confidence grows naturally. Momentum creates emotional energy. Small wins strengthen discipline.

This is why starting matters so much.

Even modest extra payments can begin shifting mindset and behavior positively. Over time, homeowners often become increasingly disciplined simply because they see evidence that their efforts are working. Community and support can also strengthen long-term consistency. Spouses, family members, financial mentors, or accountability partners may help reinforce focus during difficult periods. Mortgage acceleration becomes easier when everyone involved understands and supports the larger vision.

Communication matters especially for married couples. Financial stress and misalignment can damage motivation significantly. Couples who discuss goals openly and celebrate progress together often experience stronger long-term success.

Another overlooked source of motivation is recognizing how uncommon disciplined financial behavior actually is. Most people never fully control their debt. Many remain trapped in cycles of consumption, refinancing, and financial pressure for decades.

Homeowners who pursue intentional mortgage acceleration are building a level of financial freedom that relatively few people achieve. Recognizing this can strengthen confidence during difficult moments.

The journey itself often changes homeowners profoundly. Over time, many people discover that the habits developed during mortgage payoff—discipline, patience, delayed gratification, intentionality, and resilience—improve every area of financial life. By the time many borrowers finally eliminate their mortgage, they are no longer the same people financially. Their relationship with money has matured. Their understanding of wealth has evolved. Their confidence has strengthened.

And perhaps most importantly, they realize the process was never only about the mortgage.

It was about building a life with greater ownership, flexibility, peace, and freedom.

Mortgage payoff is not a sprint.

It is a long-term transformation built one consistent decision at a time.

And every payment moves the future closer.

How Small Consistent Payments Create Massive Long-Term Results

Let's look at a realistic example showing how staying consistent with even modest mortgage acceleration strategies over time can completely transform long-term financial outcomes.

Original Mortgage Scenario

A homeowner purchases a home with:

- Loan Amount: $375,000
- Interest Rate: 6.5% fixed
- Loan Term: 30 years
- Monthly Principal & Interest Payment: Approximately $2,370

Standard Mortgage Outcome

If the homeowner follows the normal 30-year payment schedule:

- Total Payments Over 30 Years: $2,370 × 360 = $853,200
- Total Interest Paid: $853,200 – $375,000 = $478,200

This means the borrower pays nearly half a million dollars in interest over the life of the mortgage.

Consistent Mortgage Acceleration Plan

Now imagine the homeowner commits to the following long-term strategy:

Step 1 — Biweekly Payments

Instead of paying monthly:

- $2,370 monthly

The homeowner pays:

- $1,185 every two weeks

This creates:

- 13 full payments annually instead of 12.

Step 2 — Small Extra Principal Payments

The homeowner also adds:

- $200 extra principal monthly

Step 3 — Annual Tax Refund Contribution

Every year:

- $3,500 tax refund applied toward principal

Additional Annual Principal Reduction

Extra Payment from Biweekly Structure

Approximately:

- $2,370 annually

Extra Monthly Principal

- $200 × 12 = $2,400 annually

Tax Refund Contribution

- $3,500 annually

Total Additional Principal Per Year

Approximately:

- $8,270 annually toward acceleration

Estimated Results

Instead of:

- 30 years of payments

The homeowner may pay off the mortgage in approximately:

- 19–20 years

Years Eliminated

- Roughly 10–11 years removed from the mortgage timeline

Interest Savings

Instead of paying:

- Approximately $478,200 in interest

The homeowner may pay closer to:

- Around $230,000–$260,000 total interest

Estimated Interest Saved

Approximately:

- $220,000–$250,000+ saved

Future Investment Opportunity

Now imagine the homeowner continues investing the old mortgage payment after payoff.

If they invest:

- $2,370 monthly
- For the next 10 years after mortgage payoff

- At an average 8% annual investment return

Potential investment growth may exceed:

- $430,000–$500,000+

Long-Term Financial Difference

By simply staying consistent with:

- Biweekly payments
- Small extra principal contributions
- Annual lump-sum reductions

The homeowner potentially creates:

- Hundreds of thousands in interest savings
- Earlier financial freedom
- Massive future investing power

And importantly, none of these results required:

- Extreme income
- Massive inheritance
- Lottery winnings

- Unrealistic sacrifice

The transformation came from:

- Patience
- Consistency
- Long-term discipline
- Staying motivated long enough for compounding to work.

Chapter 9

Balancing Mortgage Payoff with Investing and Long-Term Wealth Building

One of the most important financial questions homeowners eventually face is whether they should focus aggressively on paying off their mortgage early or prioritize investing for long-term wealth creation instead. This debate has existed for decades among financial advisors, investors, homeowners, and economists because both approaches offer significant advantages depending on the situation. Understanding how to balance mortgage payoff with investing is critical because the decision can dramatically influence long-term financial outcomes, lifestyle flexibility, emotional security, and retirement readiness.

Many homeowners initially approach mortgage acceleration emotionally. The idea of becoming debt-free feels powerful because it represents security, ownership, and reduced financial pressure. Eliminating a mortgage payment can transform monthly cash flow and create tremendous peace of mind. However, others argue that investing excess funds instead of aggressively paying down low-interest debt may create higher long-term wealth because investments have historically generated returns greater than many mortgage interest rates.

The truth is that this is not always an either-or decision.

The most financially successful homeowners often learn how to balance both strategies intelligently. Instead of viewing mortgage payoff and investing as competing goals, they create systems where debt reduction and wealth-building work together simultaneously.

To understand this balance properly, homeowners must first recognize the difference between guaranteed returns and potential returns. Every extra principal payment toward a mortgage creates a guaranteed return equal to the mortgage interest rate saved. For example, if a homeowner has a 6.5% mortgage interest rate, every additional principal payment effectively produces a guaranteed 6.5% interest savings on that amount over time.

This is important because guaranteed returns carry emotional and financial value. Reducing debt lowers future obligations, decreases risk, and improves stability regardless of market conditions. Investing, on the other hand, involves variable returns. Historically, stock markets, businesses, real estate investments, and retirement accounts have often produced higher long-term returns than mortgage interest rates. However, investments also involve volatility, uncertainty, and emotional risk. Markets fluctuate. Returns are not guaranteed.

This creates an important distinction between mathematical optimization and emotional comfort.

Some homeowners feel tremendous peace knowing they are eliminating debt aggressively. Others feel more comfortable building investment portfolios while maintaining manageable mortgage debt. Neither approach is universally correct for every person because personal finance is deeply connected to psychology, risk tolerance, age, family responsibilities, and long-term goals.

One of the biggest mistakes homeowners make is adopting extreme positions without considering their overall financial picture. Some people become obsessed with paying off their mortgage at the expense of retirement savings, investment opportunities, liquidity, or business growth. Others focus entirely on investing while carrying excessive debt and high financial stress.

Balance usually creates stronger long-term outcomes.

For example, a homeowner with a low-interest mortgage and no retirement savings may benefit from directing some extra cash flow toward tax-advantaged retirement accounts rather than sending every available dollar toward principal reduction. Employer matching contributions alone can sometimes produce immediate returns that exceed mortgage interest savings significantly.

On the other hand, a homeowner carrying high-interest mortgage debt while feeling overwhelmed by financial obligations may benefit psychologically and financially from accelerated payoff even if theoretical investment returns could potentially be higher elsewhere.

Financial decisions should support both wealth creation and emotional stability.

One of the most effective approaches is creating a "split strategy." Under this system, homeowners allocate extra cash flow across multiple priorities simultaneously:

- Mortgage acceleration
- Retirement investing
- Emergency savings
- Investment accounts
- Lifestyle flexibility

This balanced structure prevents financial neglect in any one area while still creating long-term momentum.

For example, a homeowner with an extra $1,500 monthly may choose to allocate:

- $500 toward extra mortgage principal
- $500 toward retirement investments
- $300 toward brokerage or business investments
- $200 toward additional savings or flexibility

Over time, this creates both accelerated debt reduction and investment growth simultaneously.

Another major factor influencing the mortgage-versus-investing decision is interest rates. During periods of very low mortgage rates, some financially disciplined homeowners may prioritize investing excess funds because potential long-term investment returns could substantially exceed borrowing costs. Conversely, higher mortgage rates increase the guaranteed savings created by accelerated principal reduction.

For example:

- Paying off a 7% mortgage produces a much stronger guaranteed return than paying off a 2.5% mortgage.

This does not automatically mean investing is always superior at lower rates or inferior at higher rates. It simply means the balance between the two becomes more mathematically significant.

Age and retirement timeline also matter tremendously. Younger homeowners with decades until retirement may prioritize investment growth more aggressively because compound investing has longer to work. Older homeowners approaching retirement often prioritize reducing fixed expenses and increasing cash flow stability by eliminating mortgage debt sooner.

A retired homeowner without a mortgage payment may require dramatically less monthly income to maintain financial security. Lower expenses reduce pressure on retirement withdrawals and investment portfolios during market downturns.

Another important consideration is liquidity. Mortgage acceleration converts cash into home equity, which is less liquid than cash savings or investment accounts. While equity creates ownership value, it may not be immediately accessible without refinancing, selling, or borrowing.

This is why maintaining emergency reserves remains essential even for homeowners aggressively reducing debt. Financial flexibility matters because life circumstances can change unexpectedly.

Some homeowners also use investing to indirectly support future mortgage payoff. Instead of sending every extra dollar toward principal immediately, they build investment accounts capable of eventually eliminating the mortgage in larger lump sums later. This approach may work well for disciplined investors comfortable managing market fluctuations.

However, this strategy requires emotional discipline because investment markets do not move consistently upward every year. Homeowners pursuing this approach must remain focused during periods of volatility rather than reacting emotionally to short-term fluctuations.

Real estate investing can also complement mortgage payoff strategies. Some homeowners intentionally balance primary residence debt reduction with acquiring cash-flowing rental properties. Rental income may eventually cover mortgages, accelerate wealth creation, and increase future flexibility simultaneously.

This demonstrates an important principle: mortgages themselves are not inherently bad. Debt becomes dangerous primarily when it lacks strategic purpose or becomes unmanageable. Controlled debt attached to appreciating assets and strong cash flow may support long-term wealth when managed intelligently.

Another critical concept is opportunity cost. Every dollar directed toward mortgage payoff is a dollar unavailable for other uses. At the same time, every dollar invested elsewhere continues allowing mortgage interest accumulation to persist longer. Financial decisions always involve tradeoffs.

The goal is not perfection.

The goal is alignment between financial behavior and long-term priorities.

One reason many financially successful individuals balance mortgage acceleration with investing is because both systems compound over time. Extra principal payments reduce future interest. Investments potentially increase future wealth. Together, they create dual momentum.

This combination can become extremely powerful over decades.

For example, a homeowner who accelerates their mortgage while simultaneously investing consistently may eventually reach a point where:

- The mortgage is eliminated years early
- Retirement accounts have compounded significantly
- Investments generate passive income
- Monthly obligations decline dramatically

This creates extraordinary flexibility later in life.

Another important psychological advantage of balancing strategies is sustainability. Homeowners who pursue only aggressive debt reduction sometimes experience burnout because the process feels restrictive. Including investing and future wealth-building often creates stronger motivation because homeowners see growth occurring simultaneously in multiple areas.

Watching investments grow while debt shrinks creates reinforcing momentum.

Technology has made balancing these strategies easier than ever before. Retirement calculators, mortgage payoff tools, investment platforms, and budgeting systems allow homeowners to model countless scenarios and optimize allocations according to their goals.

Some homeowners discover that the emotional peace created

by mortgage reduction outweighs purely mathematical investing considerations. Others feel energized watching investment portfolios grow while carrying manageable debt. Personal preferences matter because long-term financial success depends heavily on emotional consistency.

Another overlooked benefit of mortgage payoff is risk reduction. Debt increases vulnerability during economic uncertainty because required payments continue regardless of income disruptions or market conditions. Reduced debt strengthens resilience.

A homeowner without a mortgage payment may survive financial downturns far more comfortably than someone carrying heavy obligations despite strong investment balances. Cash flow flexibility creates security.

At the same time, investing remains essential because inflation steadily reduces purchasing power over time. Homeowners focused exclusively on debt elimination without building investments may eventually struggle with long-term wealth growth or retirement preparation.

This is why balance matters so much.

Financial freedom usually comes not from one isolated strategy, but from combining multiple intelligent systems together:

- Debt reduction
- Investing
- Cash flow management
- Savings discipline
- Asset growth
- Risk management

When these systems work together, homeowners create powerful long-term momentum.

Ultimately, the decision between mortgage payoff and investing is not purely mathematical. It is deeply personal. The correct approach depends on:

- Risk tolerance
- Age
- Family goals
- Retirement timeline

- Income stability
- Emotional preferences
- Investment knowledge
- Interest rates
- Lifestyle priorities

The most important thing is intentionality.

Homeowners who consciously direct cash flow toward both debt reduction and wealth-building often create far stronger outcomes than those drifting passively through decades of financial decisions without a clear strategy.

Every extra principal payment strengthens ownership.

Every investment contribution strengthens future opportunity.

And together, those decisions gradually build a life with greater flexibility, security, and freedom.

Balancing Mortgage Payoff and Investing for Long-Term Wealth

Let's compare two realistic financial approaches to understand how balancing mortgage acceleration and investing can create powerful long-term results.

Original Mortgage Scenario

A homeowner purchases a home with:

- Loan Amount: $500,000
- Interest Rate: 6% fixed
- Loan Term: 30 years
- Monthly Principal & Interest Payment: Approximately $2,998

Standard Mortgage Outcome

If the homeowner follows the standard mortgage schedule:

- Total Payments Over 30 Years: $2,998 × 360 = $1,079,280
- Total Interest Paid: $1,079,280 – $500,000 = $579,280

Scenario A — Aggressive Mortgage Payoff Only

The homeowner applies:

- $2,000 extra monthly toward principal

Total Monthly Payment

- $2,998 regular payment
- $2,000 extra principal = $4,998 monthly total

Estimated Results

Mortgage payoff timeline:

- Approximately 11–12 years

Interest Paid

Estimated:

- Approximately $180,000–$220,000 total interest

Interest Savings

Compared to the original mortgage:

- Approximately $350,000–$400,000 saved

Scenario B — Balanced Mortgage + Investing Strategy

Instead of putting the entire extra $2,000 toward the mortgage, the homeowner uses a split strategy:

Monthly Allocation

- $1,000 extra toward mortgage principal

- $1,000 invested monthly into retirement/investment accounts

The homeowner also:

- Uses biweekly mortgage payments
- Invests consistently for the full payoff period

Mortgage Results Under Balanced Strategy

Mortgage payoff timeline:

- Approximately 16–17 years instead of 30 years

Interest Paid

Estimated:

- Approximately $300,000–$340,000 total interest

Interest Savings

Compared to the standard mortgage:

- Approximately $240,000–$280,000 saved

Investment Growth

Now let's look at the investment side.

The homeowner invests:

- $1,000 monthly
- For approximately 16 years
- At an average 8% annual return

Potential Investment Account Value

Estimated:

- Approximately $420,000–$500,000+

Combined Wealth Position

By year 16–17:

Scenario A

- Mortgage fully paid off
- No investment growth during payoff years
- Huge interest savings achieved

Scenario B

- Mortgage also fully paid off several years early
- Significant interest savings achieved

- Investment portfolio potentially approaching half a million dollars

Additional Long-Term Advantage

After the mortgage is eliminated under Scenario B, the homeowner now invests:

- The old mortgage payment of approximately $2,998 monthly PLUS
- The existing $1,000 investment contribution

Total future investment contribution:

- Nearly $4,000 monthly

Over the next 10 years at 8% annual growth:

Potential future portfolio growth:

- Well over $750,000–$1 million+ additional accumulation

Key Lesson

Both strategies dramatically improve long-term financial outcomes compared to making only standard mortgage payments.

However, balancing:

- Mortgage acceleration AND
- Long-term investing

May create:

- Earlier financial freedom
- Lower interest costs
- Strong investment growth
- Greater retirement flexibility
- Better long-term wealth diversification

The most important takeaway is this:

Financial freedom is often built most powerfully when debt reduction and wealth-building systems work together rather than competing against each other.

Chapter 10

The Ultimate Mortgage Payoff Game Plan: Combining All Strategies Into Financial Freedom

Reaching the final stage of mortgage payoff strategy is not about discovering a single magical technique that suddenly eliminates debt. Instead, it is about integrating everything learned throughout the journey into a unified, sustainable, and intelligent system. The most successful homeowners do not rely on one isolated approach such as biweekly payments, extra principal reductions, refinancing, or investing alone. Instead, they combine multiple strategies into a long-term game plan that adapts over time as income, expenses, and life circumstances evolve.

The ultimate mortgage payoff game plan is built on one core principle: control. Homeowners who successfully eliminate their mortgage early are not necessarily those with the highest income or the most aggressive short-term behavior. They are the ones who take consistent control over cash flow, interest reduction, payment timing, and long-term financial decision-making. At its core, a mortgage is simply a structured debt system designed to generate long-term interest for the lender while spreading payments over time for the borrower. However, within that structure exists flexibility. Most homeowners are never taught how much control they actually have over the speed of payoff. Once they understand that control exists, everything changes.

The ultimate strategy begins with a strong foundation: the biweekly mortgage payment system. This provides the baseline acceleration effect by effectively creating one extra payment per year. On its own, this strategy may shorten the mortgage by several years and reduce interest significantly over time. However, it is only the starting point, not the final solution.

The next layer involves consistent extra principal contributions. These may come from small monthly additions, occasional lump sums, tax refunds, bonuses, commissions, or side income. The key is consistency rather than perfection. Even modest contributions applied regularly can dramatically reduce the amortization timeline because of how interest is calculated on remaining principal balances.

The third layer involves cash flow optimization. This means improving the difference between income and expenses in a sustainable way. Instead of focusing only on cutting expenses aggressively, homeowners can also focus on increasing income through side businesses, career advancement, consulting, rental properties, or investment income. The goal is not just to reduce spending but to increase the gap between income and obligations.

Once this gap expands, homeowners gain flexibility. That flexibility becomes the fuel for accelerated mortgage payoff.

The fourth layer involves strategic use of windfalls. Many households receive irregular income throughout the year such as tax refunds, bonuses, inheritance, profit distributions, or unexpected financial gains. Instead of allowing these funds to disappear into lifestyle inflation, they can be partially or fully directed toward mortgage principal reduction.

This is where many homeowners experience dramatic acceleration. A single lump-sum payment applied early in the loan term can eliminate years of future interest because it permanently reduces the principal balance on which all future interest is calculated.

The fifth layer is psychological discipline. Without emotional consistency, even the best financial strategy fails. Mortgage payoff is a long-term process that requires patience during slow early progress and discipline during financial temptations. Emotional control is what allows strategies to remain consistent over decades rather than months. Many homeowners start strong but lose momentum when life becomes busy or when progress feels slow. The ultimate game plan accounts for this by relying on systems, automation, and habits rather than motivation alone. Automatic biweekly payments, scheduled transfers, and structured budgeting reduce reliance on daily decision-making.

The sixth layer is financial balance. One of the most important lessons in the entire mortgage payoff journey is that aggressive debt reduction must be balanced with liquidity, investing, and risk management. A homeowner who eliminates debt but lacks emergency savings or retirement planning may still face financial stress later in life.

The ultimate strategy ensures that while mortgage acceleration is happening, other financial pillars remain strong:

- Emergency reserves remain intact
- Retirement contributions continue
- Investment accounts grow steadily
- Cash flow remains flexible

This balanced structure creates long-term sustainability.

The seventh layer is strategic investing. Once homeowners understand that mortgage payoff and investing are not mutually exclusive, they can begin combining both systems intelligently. Some extra income may go toward principal reduction while other portions are invested for long-term growth.

Over time, this creates a dual-compounding effect:

- Mortgage balance decreases
- Investment portfolio increases

Eventually, homeowners reach a crossover point where financial freedom becomes self-sustaining.

The eighth layer is timing awareness. Not all stages of a mortgage should be treated equally. Early years of a mortgage are extremely powerful for principal reduction because interest savings compound over a longer remaining term. Later years may shift toward investing or liquidity depending on financial goals. Understanding timing allows homeowners to allocate resources more efficiently.

The ninth layer is adaptability. Life rarely remains stable for decades. Income changes, family growth, career transitions, market cycles, and unexpected events all influence financial strategy. The ultimate mortgage payoff game plan must be flexible enough to adjust without collapsing entirely. For example, during high-income periods, homeowners may accelerate aggressively. During lower-income periods, they may temporarily reduce extra payments while maintaining baseline structure. The key is continuity rather than perfection.

The tenth and final layer is long-term vision. Mortgage payoff is not simply about eliminating a debt. It is about designing a financial life with greater freedom, flexibility, and opportunity. When the mortgage is eliminated, monthly cash flow expands dramatically, often creating new possibilities such as early retirement, entrepreneurship, travel, or increased investing.

The ultimate game plan is therefore not just a debt strategy. It is a life strategy.

Homeowners who combine all these layers create a system where:

- Debt decreases consistently
- Wealth increases steadily
- Risk is managed intelligently
- Cash flow improves over time
- Financial stress declines
- Freedom expands gradually

The result is not just a paid-off home, but a fundamentally transformed financial future.

The most powerful realization is that mortgage freedom is not achieved through one dramatic action. It is achieved through hundreds of small, intentional decisions made consistently over many years. When those decisions are aligned and structured properly, they create extraordinary results that far exceed what most homeowners initially believe is possible.

The ultimate mortgage payoff game plan is simply this: build a system that works quietly in the background while life continues forward, allowing time, discipline, and compounding to do the heavy lifting.

And over time, that system changes everything.

The Complete Integrated Mortgage Payoff Strategy in Action

Let's look at a realistic scenario showing how combining all mortgage payoff strategies creates maximum financial acceleration.

Mortgage Scenario

A homeowner purchases a property with:

- Loan Amount: $600,000
- Interest Rate: 6.25% fixed
- Loan Term: 30 years
- Monthly Principal & Interest Payment: Approximately $3,696

Standard Mortgage Outcome

If no acceleration strategies are used:

- Total Payments Over 30 Years: $3,696 × 360 = $1,330,560
- Total Interest Paid: $1,330,560 – $600,000 = $730,560

Integrated Payoff Strategy

The homeowner applies a full combined system:

Step 1 – Biweekly Payments

- $1,848 every two weeks
- Creates 13 payments per year instead of 12

Step 2 — Extra Monthly Principal

- $600 extra monthly toward principal
- $7,200 annually

Step 3 — Annual Bonus

- $10,000 annual bonus applied to principal

Step 4 — Tax Refund Contribution

- $5,000 annually toward principal

Step 5 — Side Income

- $1,000 monthly side income
- $12,000 annually toward mortgage

Total Additional Principal Per Year

Biweekly Effect

- Approximately $3,696 annually

Extra Monthly Payments

- $7,200 annually

Bonus

- $10,000 annually

Tax Refund

- $5,000 annually

Side Income

- $12,000 annually

Total Annual Acceleration

Approximately:

- $37,896 extra principal per year

Estimated Results

Instead of:

- 30 years

The homeowner achieves payoff in approximately:

- 13–14 years

Interest Savings

Instead of paying:

- $730,560 in interest

The homeowner may pay closer to:

- $250,000–$300,000 total interest

Estimated Interest Saved

Approximately:

- $430,000–$480,000+ saved

Long-Term Wealth Effect After Payoff

After mortgage elimination, the homeowner now invests:

- $3,696 monthly (old mortgage payment)
- $1,000 monthly side income now redirected = $4,696 monthly investing

Over 10 years at 8% return

Potential investment value:

- Approximately $800,000–$950,000+

Final Financial Outcome

By combining:

- Biweekly payments
- Extra monthly principal
- Bonuses
- Tax refunds
- Side income
- Consistent discipline

The homeowner achieves:

- Mortgage freedom nearly 15–16 years early
- Hundreds of thousands saved in interest
- Nearly $1 million+ in long-term investment potential

Key Lesson

The ultimate mortgage payoff result is not created by one strategy.

It is created by combining:

- Timing
- Discipline

- Income growth
- Consistency
- Cash flow optimization
- Strategic investing

When all systems work together, the mortgage stops being a long-term burden and becomes a structured path toward accelerated financial freedom and long-term wealth creation.

Final Tips and Suggestions for Mortgage Freedom

Reaching the end of a mortgage payoff and wealth acceleration journey is not just about understanding strategies—it is about mastering execution over time. Many homeowners learn the concepts of biweekly payments, extra principal reductions, refinancing optimization, and cash flow management, but only a smaller group actually reaches full mortgage freedom. The difference is rarely intelligence. It is consistency, structure, and the ability to stay disciplined long enough for compounding results to fully materialize.

Mortgage freedom is not a single financial event. It is the result of hundreds of small decisions that align with one long-term objective: reducing debt efficiently while maintaining financial stability. The final stage of this journey is about refining those decisions into a system that can be sustained regardless of income changes, economic conditions, or personal circumstances.

One of the most important final principles is sustainability. Many homeowners become overly aggressive at the beginning of their mortgage payoff journey. They reduce lifestyle spending too drastically, eliminate all flexibility, and attempt to accelerate debt payoff as quickly as possible. While enthusiasm is helpful, unsustainable strategies often fail over long periods of time. The most successful homeowners are those who build systems they can maintain for 10, 15, or even 20 years without burnout.

Sustainability means balancing progress with life enjoyment. Mortgage freedom should improve quality of life, not diminish it. Homeowners who remain too restrictive often abandon their strategy when unexpected expenses arise or when emotional fatigue builds. A better approach is steady, consistent acceleration that does not compromise basic living comfort or financial security.

Another key principle is automation. One of the strongest predictors of long-term success in mortgage payoff is whether the system operates automatically in the background. Human motivation naturally fluctuates. Life becomes busy. Unexpected expenses arise. Emotional decisions can interfere with long-term planning. Automation solves this problem by removing the need for constant decision-making.

Setting up automatic biweekly payments, scheduled extra principal transfers, and recurring savings contributions ensures progress continues even when attention shifts elsewhere. Automation transforms mortgage payoff from an active effort into a background system that operates continuously. Consistency is more important than intensity. A homeowner who makes small extra payments every month for 15 years will often outperform someone who makes large but inconsistent payments driven by occasional motivation. Financial compounding rewards consistency over dramatic bursts of effort.

Another important final tip is to always protect liquidity. One of the most common mistakes in mortgage acceleration is overcommitting available cash toward principal reduction at the expense of emergency savings. While reducing debt is important, liquidity ensures stability during unexpected events such as medical emergencies, job changes, or economic downturns.

A strong financial foundation includes both debt reduction and cash reserves. Mortgage freedom is not just about eliminating a loan—it is about building resilience. Homeowners who maintain emergency savings while accelerating mortgage payoff create a safer, more balanced financial structure.

It is also essential to recognize when to accelerate and when to slow down. Financial life is not static. There will be periods of high income where aggressive principal reduction makes sense. There will also be periods of lower income or higher expenses where maintaining baseline payments is more appropriate. Flexibility ensures long-term survival of the strategy.

Another powerful tip is to continuously redirect lifestyle inflation into wealth-building. As income grows over time, many people naturally increase spending without realizing it. Larger homes, upgraded vehicles, frequent dining out, and lifestyle improvements can absorb income increases completely, leaving no real financial progress.

Instead, homeowners pursuing mortgage freedom should consciously redirect a portion of every income increase toward debt reduction or investing. Even a small percentage of raises, bonuses, or side income can significantly accelerate long-term results when applied consistently.

It is also important to track progress visually. Mortgage payoff is a long journey, and without visible progress, motivation can fade. Regularly reviewing amortization schedules, updated payoff timelines, and interest savings helps reinforce discipline. Seeing years removed from a mortgage creates psychological momentum that strengthens long-term commitment.

Celebrating milestones is another often-overlooked strategy. Mortgage freedom should not feel like a punishment. Recognizing progress along the way helps maintain motivation. Milestones such as reducing principal by $50,000, eliminating 5 years of loan time, or reaching 50% equity can reinforce the sense of progress and achievement.

Another critical tip is to avoid comparison. Many homeowners lose focus by comparing their financial journey to others. Social media, friends, neighbors, and colleagues often present distorted financial realities. Some people appear wealthy but carry high levels of debt. Others appear modest but are financially free.

The only comparison that matters is personal progress over time. Mortgage freedom is a private financial journey, not a competition.

Homeowners should also regularly reassess their overall financial strategy. Mortgage payoff is only one component of wealth building. Retirement planning, investment growth, insurance protection, tax strategy, and business development all play important roles in long-term financial health. The goal is not to eliminate mortgage debt at the expense of everything else, but to integrate it into a complete financial system.

One of the most powerful final suggestions is to think beyond the mortgage itself. Eliminating a mortgage is not the end goal. It is the beginning of a new financial phase. Once monthly mortgage payments are gone, that cash flow becomes available for investing, business expansion, retirement acceleration, or lifestyle improvement.

For example, a $3,000 monthly mortgage payment eliminated early becomes $36,000 per year in additional cash flow. Over time, that freed-up capital can compound into significant wealth if redirected intelligently.

Homeowners should begin planning for this transition long before the mortgage is fully paid off. Having a clear post-mortgage strategy ensures that financial momentum does not stop once the debt is eliminated.

Another final suggestion is to remain emotionally detached from short-term fluctuations. Financial journeys often include unexpected expenses, market changes, income variations, or temporary setbacks. These events should not derail long-term strategy. The key is maintaining focus on the overall direction rather than reacting emotionally to temporary challenges.

Flexibility and discipline must coexist. Discipline ensures consistency. Flexibility ensures survival.

It is also important to continue learning throughout the process. Mortgage strategies, financial tools, tax laws, investment opportunities, and economic conditions evolve over time. Staying informed allows homeowners to refine their approach and improve efficiency as new opportunities emerge. Finally, the most important principle of mortgage freedom is intentional living. Every financial decision should be made with awareness of its long-term impact. Mortgage acceleration is not about restriction—it is about alignment. Aligning income, spending, savings, and investment decisions with long-term freedom creates powerful compounding results.

The homeowners who achieve true mortgage freedom are not the ones who made perfect decisions every time. They are the ones who stayed consistent, adjusted when necessary, avoided major mistakes, and remained focused long enough for time and compounding to work in their favor.

Mortgage freedom is ultimately about more than debt elimination. It is about building a life where financial stress is reduced, choices are expanded, and time becomes more available for the things that matter most.

With discipline, structure, and patience, mortgage freedom is not only possible—it is highly achievable for those willing to stay committed to the process long enough to see it through to completion.

approach and improve efficiency as new opportunities emerge. Finally, the most important principle of mortgage freedom is intentional living. Every financial decision should be made with awareness of its long-term impact. Mortgage acceleration is not about restriction—it is about alignment. Aligning income, spending, savings, and investment decisions with long-term freedom creates powerful compounding results.

The homeowners who achieve true mortgage freedom are not the ones who made perfect decisions every time. They are the ones who stayed consistent, adjusted when necessary, avoided major mistakes, and remained focused long enough for time and compounding to work in their favor.

Mortgage freedom is ultimately about more than debt elimination. It is about building a life where financial stress is reduced, choices are expanded, and future becomes more available for the things that matter most.

With discipline, structure, and patience, mortgage freedom is not only possible—it is highly achievable for those willing to stay committed to the process long enough to see it through to completion.

www.ingramcontent.com/pod-product-compliance
Lightning Source LLC
LaVergne TN
LVHW040519210926
848480LV00007BA/1515